First World War
and Army of Occupation
War Diary
France, Belgium and Germany

49 DIVISION
Divisional Troops
248 Brigade Royal Field Artillery
9 May 1915 - 31 July 1915

WO95/2782/2

The Naval & Military Press Ltd
www.nmarchive.com
Published in association with The National Archives

Published by

The Naval & Military Press Ltd

Unit 10 Ridgewood Industrial Park,

Uckfield, East Sussex,

TN22 5QE England

Tel: +44 (0) 1825 749494

www.naval-military-press.com

www.nmarchive.com

This diary has been reprinted in facsimile from the original. Any imperfections are inevitably reproduced and the quality may fall short of modern type and cartographic standards.

© **Crown Copyright**
Images reproduced by permission of The National Archives, London, England, 2015.

Contents

Document type	Place/Title	Date From	Date To
Heading	49th Division 248th Brigade R.F.A. May 1915-Oct 1916 Bde Broken U N		
Heading	War Diary of 4th W.R. (H) Brigade R.F.A. From 1-1-16 To 31-1-16 (Volume VII)		
War Diary	Hopital Farm C.R.A.S Dug-Outs B.19.C.10.1	01/01/1916	31/01/1916
Heading	War Diary Of 4th W.R. (H) Brigade. R.F.A. From 1-2-16 To 29-2-16 (Volume VIII)		
War Diary	Breilly	04/02/1916	15/02/1916
Miscellaneous	Programme of Work from 29th May 1916 to June 3rd 1916	29/05/1916	29/05/1916
Heading	War Diary of 4th West Riding (How) Brigade. R.F.A. From 1-3-1916 to 31-3-1916 (Volume IX)		
War Diary	Contay	04/03/1916	31/03/1916
Heading	War Diary of 4th West Riding (How) Brigade R.F.A. From 1-4-1916 to 30-4-1916 (Volume X)		
War Diary	Canaples	01/04/1916	30/04/1916
Heading	War Diary of 4th West Riding (How) Brigade R.F.A. From 1.5-1916 to 21.5.1916 and of 248th (W.R.) Brigade R.F.A. From 21.5.1916 to 31.5.1916 (Volume XI)		
War Diary	Canaples	01/05/1916	31/05/1916
Heading	49th Divisional Artillery. 248th Brigade Royal field Artillery June 1916		
Heading	War Diary of 248th (W.R.) Brigade R.F.A. From 1.6.1916 to 30.6.1916 (Volume XII)		
War Diary	Canaples	01/06/1916	30/06/1916
Heading	X Corps. 49th Div. War Diary Headquarters, 248th Brigade, R.F.A. July 1916		
Heading	War Diary of 248th (WR) Brigade R.F.A. From 1/7/1916 to 31/7/1916 (Volume XIII)		
War Diary	Hedauville	01/07/1916	31/07/1916
Heading	49th Divisional Artillery. 248th Brigade Royal Field Artillery August 1916		
War Diary	Mesnil (Chateau Avenue) Centre Artillery Group H.Q. Q.34.B.1.9	08/08/1916	13/08/1916
War Diary	Mesnil	13/08/1916	31/08/1916
Miscellaneous	Group Orders by Lieut. Col. H.K. Stephenson, R.F.A. Commanding Centre Group, 49th Divisional Artillery.	19/08/1916	19/08/1916
Heading	49th. Divisional Artillery 248th. Brigade R.F.A. September. 1916.		
Heading	War Diary 248th (West Riding) Brigade R.F.A. From 1-9-1916 to 30-9-1916 Volume XV		
War Diary	Centre Group H.Q. Mesnil (Q.34.B.10.95)	01/09/1916	17/09/1916
War Diary	Centre Group H.Q. Mesnil (Q.34.b.10.99)	17/09/1916	28/09/1916
War Diary	Centre Group Headquarters Mesnil (Q.34.b.10.95)	28/09/1916	30/09/1916
Heading	War Diary 248th (W.R.) Brigade R.F.A. From 1-10-1916 to 31-10-1916 Volume XV		
War Diary	Mesnil Centre Group Headqur	01/10/1916	01/10/1916
War Diary	Hedauville	02/10/1916	02/10/1916
War Diary	Grouches	03/10/1916	03/10/1916

War Diary	Saulty	04/10/1916	18/10/1916
War Diary	Orville	28/10/1916	28/10/1916
Heading	49th Division 4th W.R. Bde R.F.A. Vol II From 1-31.8.15		
Heading	War Diary Of 4th West Riding (Howitzer) Bde, R.F.A. From 1-8-15 to 31-8-15 (Volume II)		
War Diary	Elverdinghe	01/08/1915	31/08/1915
Heading	49th Division 1/4 W.R. Bde R.F.A. Vol III Sept 15		
War Diary	War Diary Of 4th West Riding (Howitzer) Bde, R.F.A. From 1-9-15 To 30-9-15 (Volume III)		
War Diary	Elverdinghe	01/09/1915	18/09/1915
War Diary	Brielen	23/09/1915	28/09/1915
War Diary		27/09/1915	28/09/1915
War Diary	Brielen	29/09/1915	30/09/1915
War Diary	Elverdinghe	19/09/1915	30/09/1915
Heading	War Diary of 10th W.R. (How) Bty 4th West Riding (Howitzer) Bde, R.F.A. From 23-9-15 To 29-9-15 (Volume I)		
Heading	War Diary Of 11th W.R. (How) Bty 4th West Riding (Howitzer) Bde, R.F.A. From 23-9-15 To 29-9-15 (Volume I)		
War Diary	Brielen	23/09/1915	29/09/1915
Heading	49th Division 4th W.R. Bde RFA Vol IV Oct 15		
Miscellaneous			
Heading	War Diary Of 4th West Riding (Howitzer) Bde, R.F.A. From 1-10-15 To 31-10-15 (Volume IV)		
War Diary	Elverdinghe	01/10/1915	31/10/1915
Heading	War Diary Of 4th West Riding (Howitzer) Bde, R.F.A. From 1-11-15 to 30-11-15 (Volume V)		
War Diary	Elverdinghe	01/11/1915	30/11/1915
Heading	1/4th W. Rig. Bde. R.F.A. Dec 1915 Vol VI		
Heading	War Diary Of 4th West Riding (Howitzer) Bde, R.F.A.from 1-12-15 To 31-12-15 (Volume VI)		
War Diary	Elverdinghe	01/12/1915	31/12/1915
Heading	49th Division 4th W.R. Bde RFA Vol I 14-5. 31.7.15		
Heading	War Diary Of 4th West Riding (Howitzer) Bde, R.F.A. From 14-5-15 to 31-7-15 (Volume I)		
War Diary	Doncaster & Venant	14/05/1915	25/05/1915
War Diary	Richbourg St Vaast	26/05/1915	29/05/1915
War Diary		09/05/1915	13/05/1915
War Diary	Richbourg St Vaast	14/05/1915	22/05/1915
War Diary	Fleurbaix	22/05/1915	27/06/1915
War Diary	Rest Area Near Bac St Maur	28/06/1915	30/06/1915
War Diary	Caestre	01/07/1915	01/07/1915
War Diary	Watau	02/07/1915	07/07/1915
War Diary	Brielen	08/07/1915	16/07/1915
War Diary	Vlamertinghe	17/07/1915	17/07/1915
War Diary	Elverdinghe	17/07/1915	31/07/1915
Heading	War Diary of 49th (W.R) Divisional Ammunition Column from 1st September 1915 to 30th September 1915 (Volume 1)		

49TH DIVISION

248TH BRIGADE R.F.A.

MAY 1915-OCT 1916

BDE BROKEN UP

Army Form C. 2118

WAR DIARY
or
INTELLIGENCE SUMMARY
(Erase heading not required.)

CONFIDENTIAL.

WAR DIARY

OF

4TH. W.R. (H.) BRIGADE, R.F.A.

FROM 1-1-16 TO 31-1-16

(VOLUME VII)

WAR DIARY
or
INTELLIGENCE SUMMARY

(Erase heading not required.)

Army Form C. 2118

Page 1

Instructions regarding War Diaries and Intelligence Summaries are contained in F.S. Regs., Part II. and the Staff Manual respectively. Title Pages will be prepared in manuscript.

Place	Date	Hour	Summary of Events and Information	Remarks and references to Appendices
HOPITAL FARM C.R.A.'s DUG-OUTS B.19.c.10.1	1.1.16 to 3.1.16		Brigade HQ moved on afternoon of Dec. 31st to C.R.A's Quarters at HOPITAL FARM handing over the Billet at ELVERDINGHE to O.C. 49th Brigade. 14th Div. (NEW ARMY) - One section each of 10th and 11th W.R. Batteries remain in action till registration of Batteries of 49th Brigade completed. On afternoon of 3.1.16 received orders from C.R.A. 14th Division to withdraw sections 10th & 11th W.R. Batteries and for this Brigade	MAP BELGIUM (B SERIES) SHEET 28 N.W.
	4.1.16 to 31.1.16		to move on the 4th, 5th, & 6th to the Rest Area and by on 4th 49 W.R. Division the Brigade marched to Rest Area, the 10th and 11th Batteries being billeted near ARNEKE (and N.N.W. of that place) and H.Q. at RUBROUCK (H.14.a.) where they remain for the 6 Brigade is now under orders to move by train northern week. Tactical exercises have been carried out and the equipment of the Brigade has been changed from 5" B.L. Howitzer to 4.5" Q.F. Howitzer. The Brigade ammunition column arrived in the Rest Area on 10.1.16 being billeted near ARNEKE (H.13 central). H.Q. Supplement to Field Marshal Sir John French's Despatches published 1.1.16 contained the names of a member of Officers and other ranks of this Brigade as worthy of "mention" and on 14.1.16 the following Honours and Awards were made. MILITARY CROSS - LIEUT. W. Eddison, J.H. 2nd Lt. Whitaker. V. 11th W.R. Battery Brigade Sergt. Maj. Seymour, T.C. Promotion - 2/LIEUT. Lord. A. to be LIEUT., 10th Battery. Distinguished Conduct Medal - B.S.M. Cotton, A.E. (10th Batty) No 877 Gunr. Driver A. 11th Batty D.C.M's (in connection with Gas ATTACK Dec.19.15) 10th Batty No 549 Bdr. Whitfield E. No 758 Gnr. RHODES J. ,, do No 616 Gnr. TENNANT, N.	MAP BELGIUM & PART FRANCE SHEET 27 1/40000

H.M. Stephenson LIEUT. COL. R.F.A.

Army Form C. 2118

WAR DIARY
or
INTELLIGENCE SUMMARY

49

CONFIDENTIAL

WAR OF DIARY

4TH. W.R. (H.) BRIGADE, R.F.A.

FROM 1-2-16 TO 29-2-16

(VOLUME VIII)

WAR DIARY or INTELLIGENCE SUMMARY

Army Form C. 2118

Page 1

Place	Date	Hour	Summary of Events and Information	Remarks and references to Appendices
BREILLY	4.2.16		The Brigade left the Divisional Rest Area on Feb. 3rd marching to BAVINKHOVE Station (near S.E. of CASSEL) and thereentraining for LONGUEAU S.E. of AMIENS, 3rd Army area; which was reached on the 4th.	MAPS AMIENS 17 / 100,000 and LENS 11 / 100,000
		A.M 8.0	The Brigade marched from LONGUEAU to billets at BREILLY on the S. Bank of the River SOMME 6 miles N.W. of AMIENS	
		P.M 5.0	Orders received from C.R.A. to move next day to billet at LA CHAUSSÉE on the N. bank of the SOMME (opposite PICQUIGNY and 8 miles N.W. of AMIENS	
	5.2.16 A.M 11.0		The Brigade marched to billet at LA CHAUSSÉE	
	13.2.16		LEFT Section 10th W.R. Battery marched to WARLOY-BAILLON 6 miles W. of ALBERT One Section Brigade Ammunition Column also marched to WARLOY-BAILLON	
	14.2.16	A.M 7.0	Right Section 10th W.R. Battery marched to WARLOY-BAILLON	FRANCE Sheet 57D S.E. 1 / 20,000
		9.0	The Brigade less one battery and one Section Amm. Col. marched to VILLERS-BOCAGE and went into billets	
		P.M 5.0	LEFT Section 10th W.R. Battery relieved a Section of the 32nd Divnl. Artillery in action at Q.33.d.7.0	
	15.2.16	A.M 5.0	The Brigade, strength as above, marched to WARLOY-BAILLON taking over billets and lines from 164 Brigade R.F.A. 32nd Div.	
		P.M 5.0	Right Section 10th W.R. Battery joined Left Section in action relieving a Section of the 32nd Divnl. Arty.	
			D Battery 164th Brigade in action W.4.c.3.7 transferred to this Brigade Battery in action grouped for tactical purposes, 10th under Southern Divn. under "Northern" Group Commander	

H.H.Stephenson Lieut. Col. R.F.A.
Comdg. 4th W.R. (Howzr.) Bde. R.F.A.

Programme of work from 21st May 1916 to June 3rd 1916

B/248th W.R. Battery R.F.A.

Monday	Time	Tuesday	Time	Wednesday	Time	Thursday	Time	Friday	Time	Saturday	Time
Battery Staff Gun Drill Signallers	9.15	Drill Order HIGH GROUND N. of MAGGOT	9.15 to 12.30	Battery Staff Gun Drill Signallers	9.15	Field Service Marching Order SOPANGO	9.15 to 12.30	Battery Staff Gun Drill Signallers	9.15 to 12.30	Fatigues & Inspection	9.15 to 12.30
Harness Cleaning SIGNALLING	2.0 pm 2.30	RIDING SCHOOL SIGNALLING	2.0 pm 2.30	Harness Cleaning & Fatigue SIGNALLING	2.0 pm 3 pm 2.30	Harness Cleaning & Fatigue SIGNALLING	2.0 pm 3 pm 2.30	General Inspection of Fatigues RIDING SCHOOL	2.0 pm 2.30	Holiday	

Major 26th 1906

F.J. ?? Major
OC Depot W.R. Battery R.F.A.

Army Form C. 2118

4 9

WAR DIARY
or
INTELLIGENCE SUMMARY
(Erase heading not required.)

Confidential
War Diary
of
4th West Riding (How) Brigade, R.F.A.

From 1-3-1916 to 31-3-1916.

(Volume IX)

WAR DIARY
or
INTELLIGENCE SUMMARY

(Erase heading not required.)

Army Form C. 2118

Page 1

Instructions regarding War Diaries and Intelligence Summaries are contained in F.S. Regs, Part II. and the Staff Manual respectively. Title Pages will be prepared in manuscript.

Place	Date	Hour	Summary of Events and Information	Remarks and references to Appendices
CONTAY	4.3.16	2.0 P.M.	In accordance with orders received from C.R.A. 1st Brigade Headquarters, 11th W.R. Battery and Brigade Ammunition Column together with the Waggon Line of 10th W.R. and D164 Batteries moved into billets at CONTAY two miles W. of WARLOY-BAILLON and 8 miles W. of ALBERT. The billets at WARLOY were taken over by the 32nd Div. ARTY.	MAPS LENS 11 1/100000 AMIENS 7 1/100000
	7.3.16		10th W.R. and D164 Batteries withdrawn from action and rejoined Brigade at CONTAY. The whole Brigade is now in CORPS Reserve.	
	15.3.16	10.0 A.M.	10th and 11th W.R. Batteries and Brigade Ammunition Column ordered to move to BEAUCOURT 2 miles S.W. of CONTAY	
		2.0 P.M.	Units named above moved to BEAUCOURT accordingly	
		3.30 P.M.	Above named units ordered to move from BEAUCOURT to HARPONVILLE 3 miles N.E. of CONTAY	
		5.0 P.M.	Above named units marched to HARPONVILLE Capt. J.E.E. Pelleran, Adjutant, proceeded to England on duty.	
	20.3.16		Capt. A. Arnold-Forster O.C. 4th W.R. Amm. Col. proceeded to England on transfer to Second Line	
	27.3.16		Brigade H.Q. and D164 Battery marched to TALMAS (10 miles N. of AMIENS)	
	28.3.16		Brigade H.Q. and D164 Battery marched from TALMAS to CANAPLES (4 miles N.W. of AMIENS). The 10th and 11th W.R. Batteries and Brigade Amm. Column marched from HARPONVILLE to CANAPLES.	
	29.3.16 to 31.3.16		In billets at CANAPLES	

H.W. Stephenson

Army Form C. 2118

WAR DIARY
or
INTELLIGENCE SUMMARY
(Erase heading not required.)

Instructions regarding War Diaries and Intelligence Summaries are contained in F. S. Regs., Part II. and the Staff Manual respectively. Title Pages will be prepared in manuscript.

Place	Date	Hour	Summary of Events and Information	Remarks and references to Appendices
			Confidential War Diary of 4º West Riding (How) Brigade R.F.A. From 1-4-1916 to 30-4-1916 (Volume X)	

1875 Wt. W593/826 1,000,000 4/15 J.B.C. & A. A.D.S.S./Forms/C. 2118.

Army Form C. 2118

WAR DIARY
or
INTELLIGENCE SUMMARY
(Erase heading not required.)

Instructions regarding War Diaries and Intelligence Summaries are contained in F. S. Regs., Part II and the Staff Manual respectively. Title Pages will be prepared in manuscript.

Place	Date	Hour	Summary of Events and Information	Remarks and references to Appendices
CANAPLES	1.4.16 to 30.4.16		During the whole month of April the Brigade was in billets at CANAPLES and engaged in training	MAP LENS No. 11 1/100,000

H N Stephenson
Lieut. Col. R.F.A.
Comdg: 42⟨W. R⟩ Bde. R.F.A.

Army Form C. 2118

WAR DIARY
or
INTELLIGENCE SUMMARY
(Erase heading not required.)

24 8 Bde RFA
Vol 10   XI

Confidential War Diary
of
4th West Riding (How) Brigade R.F.A.
From 1.5.1916 to 21.5.1916
and of
248th (W.R.) Brigade R.F.A.
From 21.5.1916 to 31.5.1916

(Volume XI)

Army Form C. 2118

WAR DIARY
or
INTELLIGENCE SUMMARY
(Erase heading not required.)

Instructions regarding War Diaries and Intelligence Summaries are contained in F. S. Regs., Part II. and the Staff Manual respectively. Title Pages will be prepared in manuscript.

Place	Date	Hour	Summary of Events and Information	Remarks and references to Appendices
CANAPLES	1.5.16 to 21.5.16		The 4th W.R.(How.) Brigade R.F.A. remained in billets at CANAPLES training till 20.5.16 when, under the pre[-]reorganisation of Artillery Scheme the Brigade with the exception of Brigade Headquarters was broken up and ceased to be a Howitzer Brigade. The 10th W.R. Battery became part of the 2nd W.R. Brigade (now 246th (W.R.) Brigade R.F.A.) under the number D/246 Battery. The 11th W.R. Battery became part of the 1st W.R. Brigade (now 245th) as D/245 Battery. D/164 Battery which in the meantime had been re-numbered the 15th W.R. Battery went to the 3rd W.R. Brigade (now 247th) as D/247. The 4th W.R. Amm. Col. became part of the Div. Amm. Col. This Brigade was renumbered the 248th (W.R.) Brigade R.F.A. and received from the 1st W.R. Brigade the 3rd W.R. Battery now A/248 Battery, from the 2nd W.R. Brigade the 5th W.R. Battery now B/248 Battery, and from the 3rd W.R. Brigade the 14th W.R. Battery now C/248 Battery. The exchange of Batteries was completed on 21/5/16.	MAP LENS No. 11 1/100,000
	31.5.16		The equipment of the Brigade is now 18 Pdr. Q.F. The 248th (W.R.) Brigade R.F.A. still in billets at CANAPLES training.	

H.K.Stephenson
LIEUT. COL. R.F.A.
COMDG. 248th. (W.R.) BRIGADE, R.F.A.

49th Divisional Artillery.

248th BRIGADE

ROYAL FIELD ARTILLERY

JUNE 1 9 1 6

Confidential War Diary
of
248th (W.R.) Brigade R.F.A.
From 1.6.1916 to 30.6.1916
(Volume XII)

Place	Date	Hour	Summary of Events and Information	Remarks and references to Appendices
CANAPLES	1.6.16 to 10/6/16		This Brigade plus B/247 Battery which was attached to it for training and discipline from the end of May, remained training at CANAPLES and acting as Divisional Reserve Artillery after the other Batteries of the 49th Div. Arty. had gone into action under the 32nd and 36th Divisions and the Xth Corps Heavy Artillery Reserve.	MAP LENS No 11 1/100000
	19/6/16		The Brigade plus B/247 Battery marched to MIRVAUX (12 miles west of ALBERT).	
	26/6/16		The Brigade plus B/247 Battery marched to HEDAUVILLE (4 miles N.W. of ALBERT) A general bombardment of the enemy trenches &c. on this front commenced on Saturday 23.6.16 and still continues – Further offensive operations are delayed by the heavy rains which have fallen during the last few days.	
	27/6/16 to 30/6/16		Bombardment continued	

HNStephenson

X Corps.
49th Div.

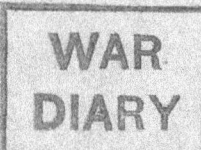

Headquarters,

248th BRIGADE, R.F.A.

J U L Y

1 9 1 6

44

Vol 13

Confidential War Diary
of
248th (W.R.) Brigade R.F.A.
From 1/4/1916 to 31/4/1916
(Volume XIII)

INTELLIGENCE SUMMARY

Page 1

Place	Date	Hour	Summary of Events and Information	Remarks and references to Appendices
HEDAUVILLE	1/7/16	A.M. 7.30 to P.M. 6.30	The 246th W.R. Brigade R.F.A. plus B/247 Battery in accordance with orders marched to a position of assembly Q.31.D. and then came under command of the 36th Division and awaited orders to take up an advanced position across the river ANCRE at Q.36.B. (South of THIEPVAL WOOD) as soon as the tactical situation permitted. The Infantry assaulted the GERMAN Trenches at 7.30 A.M. and the 36th DIVISION reached their objective. The Division on the right and left were held up though the one on the right 32nd Division with the help of the 49th Division subsequently reached its objective. The tactical situation did not however admit of this Brigade being sent forward in extension to HEDAUVILLE.	LENS 11 1/100000 Trenching FRANCE Sheet 57 D.S.E. Edition 2.B.
	2/7/16		Guns of A/248 and C/248 Batteries handed over to 32nd and 36th Divl. Artillery respectively. Guns of B/247 Battery had previously been transferred to 32nd & 36th Divns. chiefly with a view of above Divns. making good futns. of above Divn. damaged or broken down in their transfer.	C/248 ₸ Q.O.S. A
	8/7/16		B/248 Battery ordered to take over position of B/154 (36th Divn.) Battery at Q.22.1. B/248 Battery went into action same night	
	9/7/16		A/248 Battery ordered. The remaining Batteries of this Brigade and B/247 Battery ordered to relieve Batteries in action and take over their guns & positions as follows :- A/248 to relieve A/154 at Q.16.c.6.4; C/248 to relieve B/172 at Q.28.a.8.3; B/247 to relieve C/172 at Q.22.d.3.2. The Batteries went into action same night and together with B/248 formed part of Group under Lt. Col. Ward D.S.O. 36th Divl. Arty.	
	12/7/16		Artillery Group rearranged this Brigade (less Headquarters) being grouped with 246th Brigade under Lt Col. Whitley R.F.A. Comg. LEFT GROUP Authority Operation Order No 31 C.M.G.	
	18/7/16		A/248 and C/248 Batteries took over Gun positions and Guns at W.3.d.3.0 and W.11.a.3.1 respectively of Right Group.— Group Commander Lt. Col. Middleton W.11.a.3.1	

INTELLIGENCE SUMMARY

Place	Date	Hour	Summary of Events and Information	Remarks and references to Appendices
HEDAUVILLE	18/7/16		B/247 Battery ceased to be attached to this Brigade for administration and discipline.	
	19/7/16		Actg. Armr. Sgt. Maj. ALEXANDER, E.F., received Military Cross	
	24/7/16		A/248 Battery transferred to centre Group without change of position - Centre Group Commander Lt. Col. Clifford	
	25/7/16 to 31/7/16		No change in situation on this Division front	

H.W.S.Trevor

LIEUT. COL. R.F.A.,
COMDG. 248th. (W.R.) BRIGADE, R.F.A.

49th Divisional Artillery.

248th BRIGADE

ROYAL FIELD ARTILLERY

AUGUST 1 9 1 6

WAR DIARY
or
INTELLIGENCE SUMMARY

(Erase heading not required.)

Page 1

Instructions regarding War Diaries and Intelligence Summaries are contained in F.S. Regs., Part II. and the Staff Manual respectively. Title Pages will be prepared in manuscript.

Place	Date	Hour	Summary of Events and Information	Remarks and references to Appendices
MESNIL (CHATEAU AVENUE) CENTRE ARTILLERY GROUP HQ Q.34.B.1.9	8.8.16	4.0 P.M.	Under #49th Divisional Artillery orders the Headquarters of this Brigade (245th (W.R.) Bgde, R.F.A.) relieved Centre Group Headquarters (247th (W.R.) Bgde, R.F.A.) at MESNIL. A/245 Battery transferred to Left Group. The Centre Group Batteries are now A,B,C/247 Brigade B/241 Brigade (48th Div.), and D/247 (4.5 How.) for defensive purposes only. [Position of Batteries A/247 Q.22.10.20; B/247 Q.34.6.2.8; C/247 Q.22.9.1; D/247 W.3.6.3.5 in the] The Batteries of the group carried out various harassing bombardments and blocking barrages (during hours of darkness) behind the THIEPVAL – LEIPZIG SALIENT). The zone for which the group is responsible extends from R.19.c.1.6 in the NORTH to R.31.a.6.7 on the South & includes the village of THIEPVAL. The MESNIL area in shelled	TRENCH MAP FRANCE SHEET 57 D S.E. EDITION 2B
	9.8.16 to 11.8.16		intermittently day and night by the enemy.	
	12.8.16	10.30 P.M.	A, B, C/247 Batteries enfiladed enemy trenches in R.32.6 and R.33.a. in support of 12th Division attack on German trenches running from X.2 Central to R.33.a.8.2. Rate of fire 10.30 P.M. to 11.0 P.M. 6 rounds per gun per minute 11.0 to 11.30 18 rounds per gun per minute, then 12 rounds per gun per 2 minutes.	
		12.40 A.M.	Message received from H.Q. R.A. "Attack has been successful" – Rate of fire further reduced.	
		12.50	C/247 Battery reported enemy firing K (asphyxiating) Gas shell – the whole of this Group Area was shelled with this Gas filled shell none fell east of these Headquarters and the bang-bang of no inconvenience experienced here.	
	13.8.16	1.0	H.Q. R.A. at our request turned a French Batteries to persevere with Gas shell on GRANDCOURT.	

HKS

INTELLIGENCE SUMMARY

Page 2

(Erase heading not required.)

Place	Date	Hour	Summary of Events and Information	Remarks and references to Appendices
MESNIL	13.8.16	A.M. 1.5	C/247 Battery reported temporarily out of action owing to Gun shell and B/247 ordered to open C/247 Zone. Shell burst and accurate after reading.	FRENCH MAP FRANCE Sheet 57^DS.E. Edition 2B
		1.5	A/247 Battery reported gas shell burst in MESS Dug out but no one hurt. And Battery continuing in action. French Batteries opened fire and Enemy arm after caused reading	
		1.20	gas shells.	
		1.50	H.Q. R.A. ordered barrage fire to stop except Barrage from R.33.a.2.7 to R.33.B.2.7 as Infantry Patrols were going out from R.32.a.2.5 to R.32.a.5.4 - Orders given to Batteries accordingly. Batteries ordered to use guns not employed on above barrage for shooting blocked barrage &c.	
		2.15	Night Reports.	
	14.8.16		Day spent by all Batteries except B/241 (employed in action owing to trouble with Springs &c.) on usual tasks special attention being devoted to cutting wire in front of German trenches in R.19.c and R.19.a and keeping wire open already cut or remainder of zone.	
		P.M. 9.30 9.45	Bombardment by 2 Batteries of enemy trenches R.31.a.7.7 to R.25.c.7.2 for 5 minutes (4 rounds per gun per min.) then "Lift" to "APPLE TREES" (R.31.t) for 5 minutes (2 rds per gun per min.) then return to front line trenches for 2 minutes.	
			At 9.30 p.m. 146th Infy Brigade emitted smoke cloud.	
	15.8.16	10.0 to A.M. 4.0	Enemy (probably in retaliation) shelled Mesnil heavily north K Gas Shell and Shrapnel French Batteries and Heavy artillery retaliated but the retaliation was ineffective and enemy shelling continued till 4.0 a.m.	

H.K.S.

INTELLIGENCE SUMMARY

Page 3

Instructions regarding War Diaries and Intelligence Summaries are contained in F.S. Regs., Part II. and the Staff Manual respectively. Title Pages will be prepared in manuscript.

(Erase heading not required.)

Place	Date	Hour	Summary of Events and Information	Remarks and references to Appendices
MESNIL	15.8.16		A fairly quiet day. From 5 to 7.0 P.M. enemy put 12 occasional rounds 5.9 into Q.26.c and d. About 11-0 p.m. enemy shelled near Headquarters Q.34.a.with about 20 rounds 5.9's. Q.28.c. and d were also given shells	TRENCH MAP FRANCE SHEET 57D S.E. Edition 2B
	16.8.16	A.M. 11.30 to 12-0 noon	A,B, & C/247 Batteries ordered to shell approaches to THIEPVAL (Communication Trenches) with occasional bursts of fire — 85 rounds fired — Our aeroplane active all day which kept enemy artillery quiet.	
	17.8.16		A quiet day. An occasional hostile artillery fire on this area — some intermittent shelling only — Our artillery active — Aeroplane ditto.	
	18.8.16		Wire cutting barrage produced for all batteries — wire very fairly well cut but enemy (?) very fired wire or keeps rook and sandbag each night. Enemy (?) in quiet morning.	
		5.0 P.M.	In accordance with 49th Divnl Inty. Operation Order No. 194X-115 and in support of an attack by the 48th Division on their front, including D/247 (4.5" Hows.) joined in a suitable Barrage between THIEPVAL and the Leipzig attacked. The objective of the 48th Division were enemy trenches situated in X.2.a and b. The object of the 49th Division co-operating was to delay in front the garrison of THIEPVAL from forming in front of the point attacked. The attack but for a circle by the americans of a smoke cloud. In attack be entirely successful all objective being gained and over 400 prisoners taken. Artillery active HAMEL and shelled during afternoon and evening with Trench Mortar and 10 and 15 cm. Howitzers	
	19.8.16	10.7 P.M.	Enemy shelled MARTINSART — 40 rounds 10 cm + 77 mm. During the day the 25th Brinon (Air Artillery) relieved the 49th Div. (Air artillery).	

WRL

INTELLIGENCE SUMMARY

(Erase heading not required.)

Page 4

Place	Date	Hour	Summary of Events and Information	Remarks and references to Appendices
MESNIL	19.8.16	P.M.	The Distribution of 2/5th Divisional front is as follows :— **THIEPVAL AVENUE** exclusive to **RIVER ANCRE** – (1 By/Sy. Rd. & 1/2/5A Left Sector) (1 Infy. Brigade). **THIEPVAL AVENUE** inclusive to **X.2.c.25.75** inclusive Right Sector – X.2.c.25.75 inclusive to THIEPVAL AVENUE exclusive. The Left Sector is held by 2 Batts. Right Batt. from THIEPVAL AVENUE exclusive to UNION STREET R.25.a.4.3 inclusive. Batt. Hdqrs. (JOHNSTONE'S POST) Q.36.b.10.5 to UNION STREET R.25.a.4.3 inclusive Q.30.d.7.2 Left Batt. from UNION STREET R.25.a.4.3 exclusive to River Ancre – Hdqrs. GORDON CASTLE (Q.30.d.1.9). This (Centre) Group 49th Div. Arty. is in div'l support of Right Batt. Left Sector and in conjunction with LEFT GROUP of Left Sector is while the Central Group Orders No.1 dated Aug. 19.1916 incorporated with the Diary show the respective Zones covered by the Batteries composing the Group. Enemy shelled area Q.22.c. with about 50 rounds 4·2" and a few Gas shells.	TRENCH MAP FRANCE SHEET 57DSE Sheets 2B
		10·45	Enemy again shelled MARTINSART with 10 c.m. and 77 m.m. Shell about 50 from S.	
		12·0 (Midnight)	Day an unfavourable for observation till late afternoon.	
		20·8·16 5p.m.to 6 pm	Enemy artillery active all day.– From 7·40 P.M. to 8·20 P.M. enemy heavily shelled B/247 (and B/246 Gun position (and Q.34.a and Q.26.c generally) firing some 150 rounds of 5·9" shells with aeroplane observation. Though several gun emplacements and a dug-out were hit no gun was damaged. B/247 had one ass B246 two guns wounded. Enemy aeroplane were	
		P.M. 6·30	more active and our anti-aircraft gun fire ordered to day. An hour or so earlier one of our captive Balloons (observation Balloon) not ordered adrift loft up and floating towards the enemy lines. Late it burst up the Germans and began to descend – the enemy shelled and hit it – it eventually fell near MIRAUMONT according to observation of B/247 Battery. HKS	

INTELLIGENCE SUMMARY

(Erase heading not required.)

Page 5

Place	Date	Hour	Summary of Events and Information	Remarks and references to Appendices
MESNIL	22.8.16	7.30AM	Great hostile artillery activity. At 7.30 A.M. an enemy 8 inch Battery opened fire with aeroplane observation on our 6 inch (Naval with VII) Battery in Q.34.a at the bottom of MESNIL CHATEAU Avenue and continued firing till 9.0 A.M. - some 200 rounds were fired a large percentage of which were armour piercing shell with old ay action fuzes. No gun was destroyed - 2 men killed and 6 wounded - a motor lorry was burnt and the cordite in ammunition dump fired. This area was shelled intermittently all day several houses in MESNIL being destroyed with 5 in armour piercing shell.	TRENCH MAP FRANCE 57 D S.E. Edition 2 D
		6.0 P.M.	In accordance with Operation Order 49th Divl. Arty 16/AX/21 the batteries of this group including D/247 How. Battery formed an artillade barrage in R.31.a and R.31.b. This was in support of an attack by the 48th Divn whose objectives were the capture of Bivouac front and support trenches R.32.c.15, R.31.d.5.1, X.1.b.2.8, X.1.a.9.5, R.31.c.9.0, R.31.d.3.0 - 6.2.8.4. The object of the 49th Divl party cooperation area to delay the issuance of THIEPVAL from reinforcing the points attacked. All the objectives were obtained & counter attack from Pupils cooperation area was opened. 9.34 a.4.5. with 30 rounds 5.92"	
		12.0 midnight	Enemy shelled this area opening 9.34 a.4.5 and to from 6.0 to 10.0 A.M. with P.M.2.19th Shell intermittently.	
	23.8.16	8.0 A.M.	Enemy shelled areas Q.28.d and Q.34.a and 150 m.m shell with several hundred rounds of 210 mm and 150 mm shell	
		12.30 P.M. 9.30	MESNIL shelled - 20/Rds 7.7 mm shell. At request of Infantry D/247 (How) Battery fired 50 rounds retaliation on R.31.a.6.7.85 and later 18 Rds Battery fire 200 rounds on R.26.c.7.3 to R.31.a.6.3	
		9.35 to 10.20	Batteries (2 18 Pdr. & 1 How.) fired a defensive zone owing to German brigade attack	
		10.20 to	Blocking Barrage Q. Leipzig Salient and other areas night bombs, 4 Batteries	
	24.8.16	4.0 A.M.	(18 Pdrs.) 1200 rounds. This is a fair average night work for the group.	

HHS

INTELLIGENCE SUMMARY

Page 6

Place	Date	Hour	Summary of Events and Information	Remarks and references to Appendices
MESNIL	24/8/16	7.0 P.M. 4.10	O.C. coordinate with Operation Order (4th Div) Aug) 3/AX/21 the artillery of the Group supported an attack by the 25th Division from the South to gain the HINDENBURG TRENCH north of N. LEIPZIG Salient running from R.31.c.4.3 on the left to R.31.d.4.6 on the right. The attack the occurred with all the objectives being captured.	FRANCE 57D S.E. Edition 2B
		7.0 9.0 P.M.	Enemy artillery very active during the morning of the day (24th) – 7am – from MESNIL Some 300 5.9" & 8" shells fell on the area from MESNIL to MESNIL CEMETERY 9.28.d to Q.34.a. again area (9.27.d.)	
	25/8/16	5.30 A.M. to 5.0 P.M.	MESNIL shelled LONE TREE Trench junction and adjacent party in the Enemy trenches with 5.9", and 8" shells – he had a working party at work an intervals with 5.9" and 8" shells – twice which they attempted. Vicinity which had to be withdrawn a few him before day light opposite. shelled the enemies – a German Observation balloon rose up opposite LEIPZIG Salient Enemy put up a heavy barrage on our trenches from the former to THIEPVAL WOOD inclusive the HINDENBURG Trench. An intense artillery	
		5.30 A.M. to 8.30 P.M.	area in order to recapture the HINDENBURG Trench till 8.0 P.M. The batteries of the were opened on the enemy and maintained a heavy fire. The counter attack having failed. the enemy Barrage ceased. the Counter attack behind the enemy line attack. then Enemy turned an enfilade Barrage behind the enemy line shelled this	
	26.8.16	9.0 A.M.	Enemy artillery Quiet in this area except from 9.0 am to 9.30am MESNIL was shelled with 8" shells – a direct hit took off the Eastern portion of the Church Spire. Enemy	
		4.50 P.M. 8.0 P.M	Movement – about 2 R.31 central was checked by Barrage fire of this Group (1400 rounds) an unusual Blocking Barrage THIEPVAL–LEIPZIG Salient amount	
	27/8/16		Barrage at high elevation to wire cutting by all Batteries of Zone allotted to Group chiefly in R.19.C. – 1400 rounds being fired. Blocking barrage as night as usual. Enemy artillery fairly quiet.	MKS

INTELLIGENCE SUMMARY

Page 7

Place	Date	Hour	Summary of Events and Information	Remarks and references to Appendices
MESNIL	28.8.16	4.0 PM	Wire cutting same Zone on support and Reserve enemy trenches. Attack by 75th Infty. Bgde (25th Divn) on enemy trench system R.31.a.3.05 to R.31.c.7.7 (north west of HINDENBERG TRENCH) under 49th Divnl. Early Operation Order 16/AX/26. Was timed. Supported attack with one Battery B/241 with enfilade fire on trenches R.31.a.42 & 72 and R.31.a.6.5 to 9.4 - 705 rounds being fired. The attack did not succeed. Wire cutting on front, support and Reserve trenches (F.19.a and c) our Zone having on enemy have been fired by this Bgde. Hostile MESNIL town shelled intermittently all day and night. Jun. Germans with obs. were seen apparently shifting battery off... in R.2 about 6.0 P.M. During the attack by 26th Devons in R.31, F.O.O's reported many casualties among enemy guns caused by our enfilade artillery fire.	TRENCH MAP FRANCE SHEET 57 d S.E EDITION 2B and THIEPVAL 1/10000 (7.8.16)
	29.8.16	12.0 Noon	Day again chiefly devoted to wire cutting same Zone as before. 2 Enemy Aeroplanes (Fokkers) attacked 2 of our men here and brought one of our own down before MESNIL and HAMEL. Enemy Observation Baloon, up during day are frequently ascending and descending.	
	30.8.16		A wet day. Thunderstorm in afternoon. Observation difficult - MESNIL shelled intermittently during past 24 hours. Wire cutting and night tasks as usual. A good deal of enemy movement in R.25, 31 and 31.a, working parties having to be frequently dispersed by Artillery fire. The enemy did a good deal of shelling of our trenches and back areas. Wire cutting and night	
	31.8.16		Blocking barrages as usual B/246-Battery (Ore. Major Aug D.S.O joining Group - Battery position Q.35.4.3	

H.H. Sloggman
LIEUT. COL. R.F.A.
COMDG. 248th (W.R.) BRIGADE, R.F.A.

SECRET.   *** = 1 = ***   B.4.
                                Copy No. 11

GROUP ORDERS

by

Lieut. Col. H.K. STEPHENSON, R.F.A.,

Commanding Centre Group, 49th Divisional Artillery.

Reference   Sheet 57 D S.E. 1/20.000   19th August 1916.
            Xth Corps Special Map..

---

1.   The 25th Division (less Artillery) will relieve the 49th Division (less Artillery) today, 19th inst..

2.   **DISTRIBUTION OF FRONT.**

The distribution of the 25th Divisional front is as follows;
Left Sector. THIEPVAL AVENUE exclusive to RIVER ANCRE is held by the 74th Infantry Brigade.

Right Sector. X.2.c.25.75 inclusive to THIEPVAL AVENUE inclusive is held by the 7th Infantry Brigade.

The Left Sector is held by two Battalions,

(a) Right Battalion from THIEPVAL AVENUE exclusive, Q.36.b.10.5 to UNION STREET, R.25.a.4.5. inclusive.. Battalion Headquarters - JOHNSTONES POST, Q.30.d.7.2.

(b) Left Battalion from UNION STREET - R.25.a.4.5. exclusive to RIVER ANCRE. Battalion Headquarters - GORDON CASTLE, Q.30.d.1.9.

3. SUPPORTING ARTILLERY.

The Left Group, 49th Divl. Artillery commanded by Lieut Col. E.N. WHITLEY, C.M.G., T.D., R.F.A., together with the CENTRE GROUP are in direct support of the Left Sector..

The Right Group commanded by Lieut Col COLVIN, R.F.A., is in direct support of the Right Sector.

The Centre Group comprising the following Batteries covering zones as under is in direct support of the RIGHT BATTALION of the LEFT SECTOR.

A/247 Battery.   R.19.c.85.20 to R.25.b.25.60.
C/247 Battery.   R.25.b.25.60 to R.25.c.90.95.
B/247 Battery.   R.25.a.95.05 to R.25.c.80.60.
B/241 Battery.   R.25.c.80.60 to R.31.a.70.80.

For defensive purposes only.
D/247 Battery.   R.19.c.85.20 to R.31.a.70.80.

4. S.O.S.

The S.O.S. call in the Reserve Army is THREE GREEN ROCKETS discharged in quick succession and repeated at short intervals./

Sheet (2)

If more than one green rocket is seen it should be taken as the S.O.S. Signal. The S.O.S. Signal will only be sent up at points where the enemy's Infantry is attacking. This Signal should be immediately followed by a slow rate of fire - 1 round per gun per minute, between our own and the enemy's trenches. Great care must be taken where the enemy's trenches are in close proximity to our own. Fire will continue at this rate until the signal is verified by F.O.O., Battalion Headquarters or Liaison Officer with Infantry Brigade H.Q.,

IN THE EVENT OF AN ATTACK ~~EMANATING~~ on our OWN SUBSECTOR all guns will at once open at section fire 10 seconds and barrage the front line of their zones.

D/247 Battery will open on the following points at 2 rounds per gun per minute:-

    A.13.,   A.11.,   A.10.,   A.9.,

IN THE EVENT OF AN ATTACK EMANATING FROM THE LEFT 18-Pdr Batteries will open fire at section fire 15 seconds as follows:-

A/247 Battery.   One section barrage within their Battery zone.. One section enfilade zig-zag trench from ST.PIERRE DIVION to R.13.b.20.40..

C/247 Battery.   One section barrage within their Battery zone.. One section barrage Q.24.b.20.10.to Q.24.d.45.80..

B/247 Battery.   One section barrage within their Battery zone.. One section search from R.19.d.20.85 to R.14.c.05.10..

B/241 Battery.   One section barrage within their Battery zone.. One section searching communication trenches from R.19.a.50.65 to R.13.d.60.90..

D/247 (How) Battery.   B.15., B.17., B.19., at 2 rounds per gun per minute..

IF THE ATTACK EMANATES FROM THE RIGHT 18-pdr Batteries will open fire at section fire 15 seconds as follows:-

A/247 Battery.   One section barrage within the Battery zone.. One section communication trench from R.31.b.40.90. to R.32.a.15.80..

C/247 Battery.   One section barrage within the Battery zone.. One section communication trenches R.31.b.20.30 to R.32.c.20.70..

B/247 Battery.   One section barrage within the Battery zone.. One section communication trench R.31.b.00.50 to R.31.b.38.55..

B/241 Battery.   One section barrage within the Battery zone.. One section, R.32.a.20.65 to R.32.b.00.65.

D/247 (How) Battery.   On strong points B.3., B.4., B.5., B.6., B.50., two rounds per gun per minute.

5. GAS.

See Standing orders for Artillery in case of a Gas Attack by the Enemy - circulated with Special Group Orders dated 21-7-1916.
In the event of a Gas Attack on either flank tasks and rates of fire will be as laid down for S.O.S..

Sheet (3)

LOST TRENCH. See Standing orders circulated with Special Orders dated 21-7-1916.

RETALIATION. Will ordinarily be given by D/247 Battery (HOW). who will fire on junction of trenches in front and support lines as nearly as possible opposite to the part of our line that is being shelled.

AEROPLANES. If any of our aeroplanes appear to be drawing fire from the German trenches, Batteries will take the opportunity of firing at the German lines from which the fire is emanating..

F.O.Os Each Battery will keep an Officer and telephonist on duty at their respective O.P., from daylight to dark.
    A Group O.P., is established at MESNIL CHATEAU BARN, Q.28.d.85.60 which will be manned at night by an Officer and two telephonists and by day by two telephonists only, (24 hours) in Battery turn.
    The Group O.P., will be connected up with the Infantry Battalion with whom we are in direct support. It will be the duty of the Officer on duty to at once pass to Group Headquarters, Infantry calls or S.O.S. Signals, seen from the O.P..
    All O.Ps are to be in telephonic communication with the Group O.P., the latter having a switch-board and the operators there plugging the call through to whichever O.P., it is desired to call up.
    This arrangement will obviate the necessity of there being direct lines between Batteries in a Group.

10. **Liaison Officer.** Liaison Officers will be found by the Group with the Right Battalion. The tour of duty will be 48 hours. Reliefs between 2 and 5 p.m..
    A roster for this duty has been published.
    The Liaison Officer will take with him two telephonists and one telephone. He will take over from the Officer he relieves the wire from Battalion Headquarters to Infantry Brigade and from Infantry Battalion to Group O.P., and will maintain these lines during his tour of duty.
    A Liaison Officer with Infantry Brigade Headquarters will be found alternately by the CENTRE and LEFT GROUPS. Tour of duty will be four days and reliefs between 2 and 5 p.m.. This Officer will take with him two telephonists and one telephone and will be responsible for the lines to Battalion Headquarters and CENTRE Group. He will also make himself familiar with the communications of the LEFT GROUP as he is responsible for Liaison between that Group and the Infantry Brigade as well as with the Centre Group.

11. **TELEPHONE LINES.** The following wires are under the maintenance of Batteries and should be patrolled at least once daily:-

    From Battery to Group (from Battery to half distance).
    From Battery to O.P..
    From O.P. to next O.P..
    From Battery to Battery (if any).

    Each telephone line will be labelled and maintained as instructed in this Office No. B.E. 3 dated 12-8-1916.

12. This cancels Special Group Orders dated 21-7-1916 and Amendments thereto dated 25-7-1916 and 10-8-1916 which should be destroyed.

12.a. ACKNOWLEDGE.

Copy 1 O.C. A/247 Bty.   Copy 8 O.C Right Group.
    2 .. B/247 .   9 .. Left ..
    3 .. C/247 .   10 War Diary ..
    4 .. D/247 .   11 .. ..
    5 .. B/241 .   12 Retained
    6 H.Q.R.A..   13 ..
    7. G.O.C. 74th Inf.Bde. 14 ..

19-8-1916.   Capt R.F.A. & Adjt.,
                                  Centre Group, 49th Div. Artillery.

49th. DIVISIONAL ARTILLERY

248th. BRIGADE R.F.A.

SEPTEMBER. 1916.

Army Form C. 2118.

49

WAR DIARY
or
INTELLIGENCE SUMMARY.
(Erase heading not required.)

Vol 15

War Diary
248th (West Riding) Brigade R.F.A.
From 1-9-1916 to 30-9-1916.
Volume XV

WAR DIARY
or
INTELLIGENCE SUMMARY.
(Erase heading not required.)

Army Form C. 2118.

Page 1

Place	Date	Hour	Summary of Events and Information	Remarks and references to Appendices
CENTRE GROUP. H.Q. MESNIL (Q.34.B.10.95)	1.9.16		Considerable artillery and aerial activity – 8 hostile balloons up during day – enemy aircraft were several times over our line but were driven back by anti aircraft fire. Enemy artillery slow active in the area. The Batteries fired some 2000 rounds dispersal, wire cutting, harassing fire, more cutting day and night, destroying barrages & usual.	MAPS TRENCH MAP FRANCE SHEET 57 D.S.E Edition 2B 2 gds. ST PIERRE DIVION 1 5000
	2.9.16		Comparatively quiet day – Batteries engaged on usual tasks. Allied aeroplane came down near MESNIL CHATEAU (Q.28.d) on power of enemy a.a. shell fire. Pilot killed. Machine brought down. Safety observer – enemy shelled machine on ground.	
	3.9.16	5:10am	The Batteries of this Group including B/245 and B/247, aerial section C/242 attached to B/247 B/241 (which supported attack by 25th Div. in R.31), supported an attack by the 49th Division in accordance with Operation order No. 14 49th Div. Arty. No. 33. The Centre Group was in direct support of the 147th Infty. Brigade which was the right attacking Brigade. The 146 Inf. Bde was the left attacking Brigade. The limits of the Right assaulting Brigade were 1st Objective – Enemy front line R.19.c.8.4 to R.19.c.1.6 both inclusive – support line R.19.c.9.5 to R.19.c.3.8 both inclusive (2nd Objective German second line called STRASSBURG TRENCH – Attack on this was to take place Sept 4.) The left assaulting Brigade had similar objectives up to the South bank of the	

H.M.S.

Army Form C. 2118.

WAR DIARY
or
INTELLIGENCE SUMMARY.

Page 2

(Erase heading not required.)

Instructions regarding War Diaries and Intelligence Summaries are contained in F. S. Regs., Part II. and the Staff Manual respectively. Title pages will be prepared in manuscript.

Place	Date	Hour	Summary of Events and Information	Remarks and references to Appendices
				MAPS
Hd. Qrs.	3.9.16	5.10 AM. to 5.13	River ANCRE. Simultaneously with this attack the 39th Div. assaulted similar objectives immediately north of the same river while the 25th Divn.	TRENCH MAP FRANCE 57 D S.E. 1 20000
CENTREGAOUT			attacked south of THIEPVAL in R.31.C and at	Edition 2.B
MESNIL			at 5.10 a.m. the Batteries of this Group barraged the enemy front line R.19.C.9.1 & R.19.C.1.5	ST PIERRE DIVISION 1 20000
(Q.34.B.10.95)			- 18.18 Pdrs., 4 rounds per gun per minute for 3 minutes	
		5.13 to 5.18	Batteries lifted on to enemy support line which was barraged for 5 minutes at the rate of 3 rounds per gun per minute.	
		5.18 to 5.25	Barrage lifted on to enemy reserve line (STRASSBURG TRENCH) - rate of fire 2 rounds per gun per minute. - Rate of fire gradually reduced according to programme till the minimum rate of ½ round per gun per minute was reached	
		6.40	Up to this hour visibility was very bad as frost owing to the attack taking place at 6.40 AM. before the hour of daylight then owing to the morning mist rising from the river Ancre and low lying marshes and later owing to battle smoke. F.O.O's were unable to see anything and 147 D Infantry Brigade Heads quarter had no information of the progress of the assault. The enemy put up a very heavy artillery barrage on our trenches very quickly	

HKS

WAR DIARY or INTELLIGENCE SUMMARY

Army Form C. 2118.

Page 3

Place	Date	Hour	Summary of Events and Information	Remarks and references to Appendices
Hd. Qrs. Centre Group MESNIL (G.34.d.1.9.5)	3.9.16	A.M 6.30	Wounded men returning reported that the assaulting battalions of 147th Infy. Brigade had carried both enemy front and support line trenches. The Arty. Liaison Officer with this Brigade confirmed this. About the same time it was reported that the right battalion of the left Inf.antry Brigade (146th) had failed to reach enemy front line, but that the left battalion had gained its objective at all events enemy front line. This was confirmed.	MAPS TRENCH MAP FRANCE 57.d S.E. 1 20000 — Dublin 2B — 10000 St PIERRE DIVION 1 — 5000
		9.15	The enemy maintained a heavy fire on THIEPVAL WOOD	
		9.55	F.O.O. reported enemy movement and manning trenches on left	
		10.5	Hardy (147th Bde.) report our men driven back by counter attack to our own line	
		10.15	The whole of the right of 147th Brigade reported back in their own old front line.	
		10.27	In accordance with orders from H.Q.R.A. batteries of this group on orders to bombard German front line trench at 1½ rounds per gun per minute. Many stragglers and wounded seen by F.O.O.'s coming back across "No Man's Land" all day. The attacks of the 25th and 39th Divisions also failure. Various enemy trenches and communication trenches were kept under fire throughout the day. This Group had 3 casualties, including 2nd Lieut. BATER, A/247, killed.

WAR DIARY
or
INTELLIGENCE SUMMARY.
(Erase heading not required.)

Army Form C. 2118.

Page 4

Place	Date	Hour	Summary of Events and Information	Remarks and references to Appendices
Hd. Qrs. Centre Group MESNIL (Q.34.b.10.95)	4.9.16	11.0 P.M (3.9.16)	Generally in preparation for the attack enemy shelled the whole of the	MAPS — As before
		5.0 A.M (4.9.16)	MESNIL valley from Q.22 Central to Q.33 as well as MESNIL village and	
			CHATEAU area Q.26 and Q.34 (including Mine Hd. Qrs.) for five hours with great intensity using K (Prior.) Gas and Lachrymatory shells as well as ordinary shells of all calibres. — No casualties.	
		P.M. 2.10	An apparently wounded English soldier was seen to walk from German lines to "No Man's Land" and enter our trench at Q.24.d.20.15 and was not fired upon although in full view. On 10 minutes later 147th Inf Bde. reported they took over our front held by 146th and 147th Infty Brigades.	
	5.9.16		MESNIL heavily shelled all day. Enemy Shelling — 6 Batteries engaged on ordinary tanks	
	6.9.16		Do. Do.	
	7.9.16	10.45 P.M. 6.30 A.M	From 10.45 P.M. on 6th to 6.30 A.M. on the 7th the enemy shelled the whole of the MESNIL area including Mine Hd Qr. with some 500 rounds	
		A.M.	of K. Gas, Lachrymatory Gas and ordinary 5.9" & 4.2" shells. There	
		2.30 to	were no casualties in this group. From 2.30 a.m. 147th Infty Brigade	
		5.15	reported steady rate of fire on enemy trenches (front defensive zone) as our trenches were being shelled with gas shell — fire continued till 5.15 a.m.	

HKS

WAR DIARY or INTELLIGENCE SUMMARY

Army Form C. 2118.

Page 6

Place	Date	Hour	Summary of Events and Information	Remarks and references to Appendices
Hd. Qrs. Centre Group	7.9.16		In addition to usual tasks enemy roads kept open day and night and night blocking barrages as before. MESNIL area shelled intermittently throughout the day. Seen enemy observation Balloons up.	MAPS —
MESNIL Q.34.B.10.95	8.9.16	noon 12.0 to 1.30 P.M.	Enemy shelled Q.34.B. and d. with about 100 rounds 150 mm and 105 mm H.E. During the morning day several small balloons drifted from the enemy lines over this area where they came down containing copies of the "Gazette des ARDENNES" a journal printed in French and published by the Germans in allied territory occupied by them. The journal was chiefly noticeable for his manner of French prisoners in German hands.	
		7.30	An aeroplane reported by wireless Hostile Battery firing at R.26.c.34.34 and 2. 18 Pdr. Batteries were at once ordered to engage this target. Flashes	
		9.0	were again observed by B/241 F.O.O. at the same point at 9.07 P.M. at which time this area was being shelled. B/241 engaged target and shelling ceased. Batteries dispersed many enemy working parties - light tasks as usual.	
	9.9.16	P.M. 2.40	Retaliation for Infantry on enemy front trenches for their shelling of own - Bapaume?	
		4.35	In accordance with 49th Div. Arty. Order 16/AX/34 this Group in conjunction with left Group carried out bombardment of enemy front and support line trenches.	

H.K.S.

WAR DIARY or INTELLIGENCE SUMMARY

Army Form C. 2118. Page 6

Place	Date	Hour	Summary of Events and Information	Remarks and references to Appendices
Centre Brook Hd. Qrs. MESNIL (Q.34.d.10.95)	9.9.16	P.M. 5.0	In retaliation to our bombardment enemy shelled our trenches	MAPS on file
		9.0	Liason Officer with Right Battalion reported enemy shelling near Battalion H.Qrs. (JOHNSON'S POST) with Trench Mortars containing Chlorine Gas	
		11.20	At request of Infantry Brigade (148") Battery ordered to open fire on enemy Trenches in defensive zone – shrapnel & fire for ten minutes. C/248 Bty forment trench and overshelled position at W.3.b.4.7. Enemy artillery fairly quiet during day	
	10.9.16	5.15 P.M.	At the request of the Infantry 4th Battery opened fire on the enemy trenches and support zone R.25.a. and c and R.31.a on account of French Mortars firing Chlorine Gas. D/247 (How.) Battery ordered to fire on R.33.B.4.3	
		6.17	1/18th Batty 1.4.5" How. Battery aim on Trench Mortars retaliated on suspected enemy Trench Mortar positions. Night hours as usual. Considerable traffic reported all day on TREES – STEEVILLERS and GREVILLERS – ACHIET-LE-PETIT roads. MESNIL area was shelled both afternoon and evening with class of gas on Calibri	
	11.9.16		Left Battery observing fire of the 18th Bde. Shoot shelling by 2 our Artillery were observed in our area and enemy emplacements and Enemy Battery position (R.34.h.3.3) were demolished. One of D/247 Bombing hit and slightly damaged.	

HWS

Army Form C. 2118.

WAR DIARY
or
INTELLIGENCE SUMMARY.
(Erase heading not required.)

Page 7

Instructions regarding War Diaries and Intelligence Summaries are contained in F.S. Regs, Part II. and the Staff Manual respectively. Title pages will be prepared in manuscript.

Place	Date	Hour	Summary of Events and Information	Remarks and references to Appendices
Corbie Group Headqrs	11.9.16	P.M. 6.0	Bombardment of MIRAUMONT by Heavy Artillery	MAPS as before
MESNIL		7.15 A.M.	2 18 Phr. Batteries fired on to Infantry target R.32.a.3.3 reported by wireless from aeroplane	
(R.34.b.10.95)	12.9.16	10.0	A working party of the 48th Div. Arty. who by arrangement were putting 2 gun pits into empty emplacement at B/247 Battery position commenced digging from surface near the position and were much in evidence.	
		11.0	German aeroplane flying low over THIEPVAL and working with 5.9" Battery registering B/247 Battery position hitting a gun emplacement and slightly damaging one gun. Enemy more in Group 3 zone reported strengthened - Batteries re-opened 8 a.m. Retaliated on hostile Batteries	
		P.M. 5.45 8.0		
		4.0 & 7.0	Enemy heavily shelled C/247 with 300 pound 5.9" shells making 8 direct hits - 2 on one emplacement which collapsed but gun un-damaged - no casualties.	
		8.30 A.M.	MESNIL Valley shelled with 5.9" — night taken as usual	
	13.9.16	7.30	Enemy working party moving Excavator at R.31.B.40.95 fired on and dispersed	
		9.30 P.M. & 4.0 A.M.	German party again dispersed and took their apparently finally cleared	
	14.9.16	Night Jack	(Blocking Barrage) THIEPVAL - LEIPZIG Salient, keeping wire (fence) as usual	
		4.45	Bombardment of enemy front and support line chan.. 148th Infy Brigade	

HHS

WAR DIARY
or
INTELLIGENCE SUMMARY.
(Erase heading not required.)

Army Form C. 2118.

Page 8

Place	Date	Hour	Summary of Events and Information	Remarks and references to Appendices
Hdqrs. Centre Group MESNIL (Q.34.E.10.95)	14.9.16	A.M. 1.45	who made a raid on enemy front line trench which was found unoccupied.	MAPS as before
			Several enemy working parties fired on and dispersed during morning.	
		P.M. 4.35 5.40	Fired occasional rounds on enemy movement at R.25.c.9.5.4.5	
		6.30	In accordance with 49th Div. Arty. Operation order No 2.16.AX.37 & 18th Bn. Batteries fired 593 rounds on SCHWABEN TRENCH from R.32.b.7.9 to R.26.c.3.4 and area South of THIEPVAL R.25.c and d and R.26.c in support of attack by 11th Division on the line R.31.d.9.8 – WONDER WORK – R.28-b.03 – a.91-c.78. The 11th Division captured all their objectives.	
		7.20	2.18 Pdr. Balloons fired 40 rounds on enemy infantry reported by wireless at R.32.a.7.3. Light tank in view.	
	15.9.16	A.M. 6.20	In accordance with 49th Divnl. Arty. Operation order 16/AX/39 the Batteries of this Group took part in an artillery "feint" on the trenches between THIEPVAL and the river ANCRE – At the same time a general attack was made by the Fourth Army and the Canadian Corps. The artillery feint was preceded by a discharge of smoke on the 49th Div. front.	
		6.20 to 6.25	A, B, & C/247 Batteries barraged enemy frontline R.19.c.84-45-15. (Before TSPEC NOSE Moderne)	HCS

WAR DIARY or INTELLIGENCE SUMMARY

Army Form C. 2118.

Page 9

Place	Date	Hour	Summary of Events and Information	Remarks and references to Appendices
Headqtrs.				MAPS
Entre Group	15.9.16	6.25	Same Batteries barraged enemy support line R.19.C.9.5 – 8.6 – 4.7 – 3.8	As before
		6.30	Same Batteries barraged enemy Barrage line R.19.d.19 – R.19.a.63 – 54	
MESNIL		6.30	Same Batteries barrage enemy front line again	
(Q.34.b.10.95)		6.32		
		6.35	During above period B/241 and C/246 Batteries remained in observation	
		6.35	A, B and C/247 Batteries engaged hostile batteries which had been previously located	
		6.50	Enemy fairly subdued at R.25.b.6.0 and R.31.b.5.9. 1 Battery, 34 rounds	
		7.11		
		10 am onwards	Counter Battery work by all Batteries. Enemy Anti-aircraft guns – hun aeroplane carrying high flash charge.	
			Hostile Artillery quick no fire. MESNIL area bombarded all day but very little observation as	
			batteries in this area seem engaged all day in neutralizing their fire.	
	16.9.16	9.0 AM	Enemy shelled our Headquarters with 4.2 shells destroying temporary all telephone communications.	
		2.0	In accordance with 49th Divl. Arty. Operation orders 16/AX/38 2 Batteries of this Group	
			fired 265 rounds in support of raid by 148th Infty Brigade on POPES NOSE.	
		10.30	Hostile battery reported by wireless at R.22.b.5.4 – engaged by 1 Battery 26 rounds	
			Then aeroplane at 10.50 reported "O.K."	
		11.15 AM	Hun-y wire cutting by 3 Batteries at R.25, d.0.8 & R.25.b.1.3. In fire 49th Divl. Arty.	
		4.30 PM	Operation Order No 16/AX/41	

HRS

Army Form C. 2118.

WAR DIARY
or
INTELLIGENCE SUMMARY.

(Erase heading not required.)

Page 10

Instructions regarding War Diaries and Intelligence Summaries are contained in F.S. Regs., Part II. and the Staff Manual respectively. Title pages will be prepared in manuscript.

Place	Date	Hour	Summary of Events and Information	Remarks and references to Appendices
Hedges Centre Group MESNIL (Q.34.c.10.95)	16.9.16	P.M. 6.30 6.42	A) In accordance with above operation order bombardment of enemy trenches about THIEPVAL in conjunction with smoke barrage executed Infantry (4 Battn.in) 30 (R.B.) In accordance with 49th Inf. Bde. Operation Order 16/AX/42, 2 Batteries fired 192 rounds.	MAPS A. I yr
		11.10	A enemy trenches R.19.c.9.5 – 86 – 66 in support of raid by 148th Infy. Brigade. Hostile Artillery quiet in the part of the front till 3.0 p.m. after which Mn. THIEPVAL WOOD and MESNIL areas were shelled till after midnight – The Infantry about this	
	17.9.16	A.M. 2.27	hour were heard to put shell on Batteries of the Batteries (when group retaliated) On enemy trenches. B/241 Battery joined Light Group – 45me 146me. 20th Regt French Arty joined centre Group for defensive purposes only. In accordance with same Operation order. (16/AX/42) 3 Batteries fired 624 rounds.	
		8.30 9.30	in support of Raid B by 148th Infy. Brigade – The Infantry reported that this Second raid was successful and that the fire of this Group most effective. This area was intermittently shelled with 105 and 150 mm. Hows. shell which dropped round MESNIL CHATEAU, B/247 position and a far as the Cemetery (Q.34.c.3.6) Several shells dropped round shape Head quarters and there were a number of casualties – B/247 had 2 men hit and while the M.O. was dressing the wounds of one of them outside this Headquarters Cookhouse another shell burst close to wounding 4 of the men being dressed, and also 2 men of Signals working on telephone Gerner.	

H.M.S.

Army Form C. 2118.

WAR DIARY
or
INTELLIGENCE SUMMARY.

Page 11

(Erase heading not required)

Place	Date	Hour	Summary of Events and Information	Remarks and references to Appendices
Centre Broch Hedqrs MESNIL Q.34.B.10.9.9 to	17.9.16	A.M. 8.30 to 9.30 P.M. 6.30	Green (Officer Arrival) who was helping with wounded. The M.O. (Capt. Brown R.A.M.C. attached 205th (M.R.)B.3d. R.F.A.) and his Servant Driver Morehouse who was assisting him were also slightly wounded but continued the removal of all the wounded under cover and dressed their wounds before leaving their own attended to. In accordance with 49th Div. Arty. Operation Order No. 3/AX/42, 2 Batteries (A + C/247) fired 800 rounds in support of attack by 147th Infty. Brigade. The objectives of the attack was to seize and consolidate the following line:- Trench R.31.a.9.1 through R.31.c.6.9 including trench to 7.2 thence digging a new line to present German trench at about R.31.c.4.7. All three objectives were obtained. Counter Battery work in progress to wireless reports of active enemy batteries.	MAPS as before
	18.9.16	5.0 A.M. to P.M. 12.30	Enemy Artillery quiet so far as this area concerned. Night tasks - 3 Batteries 1350 rounds. 2 Batteries fired on enemy batteries at R.22.B.2.5 - R.15.0.8.5, 504 R.15.c.9.5, 90, 47 Roh.	
	19.9.16	2.0 A.M. to 10.0 P.M. 12.45	Blocking Barrage South of THIEPVAL - 2 Battery 390 rds. Occasional rounds on hostile battery at R.15.c.9.96. 1 Battery 24 rounds. The area including Thne Hedqr. shelled intermittently for about 24 hours. R.15.c.5.5 and R.15.c.9.5 - 1 Battery 40 rounds. Counter Battery work - hostile batteries at R.15.c.5.5 and R.15.c.9.5 - 1 Battery 40 rounds. MESNIL and including Thne Hedqr. shelled intermittently all day.	

HKS

WAR DIARY
or
INTELLIGENCE SUMMARY.
(Erase heading not required.)

Army Form C. 2118.

Page 12

Place	Date	Hour	Summary of Events and Information	Remarks and references to Appendices
Hogra - Centre Bmp & MESNIL (Q.34.b.10.99)	20.9.16	A.M. 8.15	In accordance with 49th Divl. Arty. Operation Order 16/AX/45, 3 batteries fired at 6.12 p.m. in support of patrol on Pt. 84 by 145th Infy. Brigade. (M.19.19.C)	MAPS As before
		11.0 P.M. to 1.0	Counter battery work on hostile batteries at R.15.c. and R.21.a. 3 batteries 12.8 rounds. Many batteries and working parties were fired upon during the day and night.	
		11.0	Area received a good deal of retaliatory fire. - From 11.0 P.M. to 12.0 midnight the enemy shelled this area with 77 mm. & 4.2" mixed with gas shell. - The day was mostly rainy and brightly hot.	
	21.9.16	P.M. 3-0	During afternoon & evening enemy working parties were dispersed. Counter battery work at R.15.c. - 1 Battery 12 rounds. From other howitzer shoot the whole of the MESNIL area especially Q.34.b. was heavily shelled with 5" (?) armour piercing 5.9 and 77 mm. shells. THIEPVAL Blocking barrage during night 445 rounds.	
	22.9.16	A.M. 7.45 to 10.25	Q.34.a. and b. heavily shelled - mostly 150 mm. Q.34.a. km again	
		12.30 to	shelled at midday. During whole afternoon continuous movement seen on road passing from L.24.a.0.0 to L.16.c.0.3. - Vehicles, cyclists and men mounted and on foot.	
		7.0	S.O.S. Signal reported from trenches on our right - Orders received from H.Q. R.A. to fire	
		7.55 to 8.15	on JOSEPH'S and SCHWABEN Trenches - 2 Batteries fired 60 rds. Situation reported quiet 8.15 HMS	

Army Form C. 2118.

WAR DIARY
or
INTELLIGENCE SUMMARY.
(Erase heading not required.)

Page 13

Remarks and references to Appendices: **MAPS**

Place	Date	Hour	Summary of Events and Information	Remarks
Hd. Qrs. Centre Group (Q.34.B.10.99)	22.9.16	P.M. 8.0	B/241 Battery rejoined Centre Group and ordered out of /248 Battery to leave present position at MARTINSART and to go into position near Railway (N.E. corner of AVELUY WOOD) at...	Maps before
	23.9.16	11.0 to 2.30 A.M.	Q.35.d. and b respectively – From 11.0 P.M. 22nd to 2.30 A.M. 23rd MESNIL & eastern entrances to MARTINSART area shelled with lachrymatory gas shells sometime at the rate of 10 rounds per minute. From 9.0 A.M. to 12.30 P.M. same	
		9.0 to 12.30 P.M.	area again shelled in similar manner –	
	24.9.16	8.0 P.M. 4.50 A.M. (24th)	THIETPVAL (Blocking)	
		5.1 P.M. 6.1 " 7.1 "	Barrage – 2 batteries 560 rds. } 9 Batteries fired bursts of fire at THIETPVAL in conjunction with Trench Mortars firing gas – as per Operation Order 16/AX/47	
		8.0 P.M.	One battery fired at report of Infantry or Enemy Road known at R.25.d. O.8	
	25.9.16	5.0 A.M.	THIETPVAL Blocking barrage 2 Batteries 1050 pounds	
		9.0 A.M.	MESNIL village and Valley (Q.28.c. and Q.34.a) heavily shelled by apparently three	
		11.0 A.M.	Enemy Batteries – three enemy aeroplanes up registering for these batteries	
		4.0 P.M.	Lost Barrage on Southern area of THIETPVAL 4 Batteries 32 rounds – light blocking bursts on Thiepval Enemy aircraft active all day.	
	26.9.16	12.35 P.M.	In accordance with 49th Div. Artly Operation order no. 35 4th Batteries of this Group supported the attack on THIETPVAL by the 18th Division. The 11th Corps in Co-operation with the CANADIAN Corps on its right attacked the ridge running from N.W. of COURCELETTE to the SCHWABEN REDOUBT (R.19.c.). The attack of the IInd Corps was carried out by the 11th Div. on the right and	

HMS

WAR DIARY or INTELLIGENCE SUMMARY.

Army Form C. 2118.

Page 14

Place	Date	Hour	Summary of Events and Information	Remarks and references to Appendices
Centre Group		P.M.		MAPS
Headquarters	26.9.16	12.35	and by the 18th Div. on the left – The 49th Div. Arty. and the 25th Div. Arty. supported the attack of the 18th Division. Dividing line between 11th & 18th Div. Well in R.32.c.7.9 to R.26.a.4.1 following line of trees through R.32.a. to point of junction of final objectives	As before
MESNIL (Q.34.B.10.d.9)			Objective – 11th Div. from STUFF REDBT. along HESSIAN TRENCH to junction with MIDWAY LANE at R.20.d.1.0. 18th Div. from R.20.d.1.0 to R.26.c.4.5. Thence along Northern edge of SCHWABEN REDBT. via R.19.d.9.9 and R.19.d.6.9 to R.19.d.3.9 (thence to German frontline trench at R.19.C.9.1 Intermediate objectives for 18th Div. (1) R.26.c.70.35 to R.26.c.3.4 to R.25.d.6.7 to German front line R.25.a.95.00 (11) from junction of trenches at R.26.a.4.1 to trench junction R.26.a.20.33. Thence along Northern outskirts of THIEPVAL via R.25.b.7.2 and 43.b. to German front line at 34.	
		12.58	Green line (1st objective) reached at R.25.d	
		1.10	THIEPVAL Chateau taken – Our infantry held up in German frontline (extreme left of advance) at R.25.c.e.7.1. 100 German prisoners seen being marched back to our line. Green line taken except Our infantry seen N. of THIEPVAL – More prisoners seen – Our infantry bombing up German front line.	Fontaine left
		1.15		
		1.45		
		3.41	Message received to send ammunition from THIEPVAL CHATEAU	
		4.46	Telephonic communication established between this group and F.O.O's at THIEPVAL	

WAR DIARY
or
INTELLIGENCE SUMMARY.

Army Form C. 2118.

Page 15

Place	Date	Hour	Summary of Events and Information	Remarks and references to Appendices
Centre Group Hdqrs. MESNIL (Q.34.8.10.9.9)	26.9.16	P.M. 4.40	CHATEAU – "Purple Line" (2nd Objective) reported captured. The "Brown Line" (final objective – SCHWABEN REDBT.) has not taken. The operation appears to go through satisfactorily but considerable opposition was met with on the entrance. But all through the afternoon. The Artillery barrage rather ran away from our Infantry who could not advance as fast as the time table of Artillery "Lifts" especially on the left. The enemy Artillery were quiet so far as the MESNIL area was concerned being too much occupied elsewhere.	MAPS as before
	27.9.16	10.0 to 7.0 AM	4 Batteries fired 1320 rounds (Blocking Barrages).	
		P.M. 12.9	The Artillery of this front was chiefly engaged during the day in firing upon enemy movement observed in various parts of R.19. At 12.9 p.m. in retaliation for enemy heavy barrage of THIEPVAL and THIEPVAL WOOD 4 Batteries were ordered to barrage enemy trenches, and again firing 48 pounds enemy barrage ceased.	
		2.45 to 3.10	In accordance with Central (Telephone) orders from H.Q.R.A. 2 Batteries were ordered to bombard enemy trenches R.19.d.9.9 & R.20.c.2.7, and R.19.d.9.2 to 6.5 and light track (Blocking Barrage) 4 Batteries fired his tasks	
	28.9.16	9.0 to 5.0	fired 400 rounds – light track (Blocking Barrage) 4 Batteries fired 1683 rounds – 12.30 h 12.45 enemy shelled vicinity of these Head quarters. HPW	

Army Form C. 2118.

WAR DIARY
or
INTELLIGENCE SUMMARY.
(Erase heading not required.)

Page 16

Place	Date	Hour	Summary of Events and Information	Remarks and references to Appendices
Corps Group Headquarters MESNIL (Q.34.C.10-95)	28.9.16	P.M.	In accordance with 49 Div. Arty. Operation Order No. 3/A/X/56 the Batteries of this Group supported an attack by the 18th Division on the SCHWABEN REDOUBT. The Infantry kept pace with the lift of the Artillery Barrage and quickly extablished the main portion of their objective. — The enemy offered a strong resistance at R.19.c.9.1	MAPS as before.
		5.57	At 5.57 the enemy was still holding out at R.19.c.4.5 and the N.E. corner of the SCHWABEN. R.19.c.65 an outside the original objective but our Infantry had bombed their way up to this point (the POPES NOSE) along the enemy front line trench (facing West) and held up to that point at the close of the day. Many prisoners were observed & F.O.Os. to be taken. During the day the Batteries of the Group fired 3843 rounds and had many opportunities of engaging parties of the enemy in the open as well as Enemy machine gun parties. At the close of the day it was announced that at the 18th Div. had obtained its objective.	
		9.0	Night blocking barrage a.m and 4 Batteries fired 1580 rounds.	
		11.30	Enemy shelled MESNIL CHATEAU, the Valley and the vicinity of these Headquarters with H.E. and Lachrymatory gas shell. The Group O.P. at the Chateau was hit several	
	29.9.16	A.M. 3.30	times one shell bursting in the telephone pit — no casualties owing to gas helmets HLE	

Army Form C. 2118.

WAR DIARY
or
INTELLIGENCE SUMMARY.   Page 17
(Erase heading not required.)

Instructions regarding War Diaries and Intelligence Summaries are contained in F. S. Regs., Part II. and the Staff Manual respectively. Title pages will be prepared in manuscript.

Place	Date	Hour	Summary of Events and Information	Remarks and references to Appendices
Ancre Group Headquarters MESNIL (9.34.b.10.95)B	29.9.16	A.M. 11.30 6.70 P.M.	The Batteries of 9th Bde.R.A. in accordance with H.Q.R.A. orders fired 386 rounds on enemy trenches — a defensive barrage — from 7.0 P.M. 29th to 6 a.m. 30th. Night tanks — 4/ 18 Pdr. Batys. and 1 4.5" How. Baty. fired 1600 rounds.	MAPS As before
	30.9.16	7.0 P.M. to 6.0 A.M. 30.9.16	During the 29th MESNIL was intermittently shelled.	
	30.9.16	A.M. 6.47	Fired a defensive barrage line — 5 Batteries 2620 rounds in response to S.O.S. call from SCHWABEN REDBT.	
		9.0	Enemy appeared to be massing in R.19 Central and also to be making & bringing down the STRASSBURG trench (German Reserve line). They were fired on with good effect. The following Hon. awards have been made:— Capt. J. GREENE R.A.M.C. (attached 248th Bgde. R.F.A.) D.C.Medal; 525 Dr. MOOREHOUSE (Officers Servant Hd.qr. 248 Bgde. R.F.A.) D.C.Medal; 1596 Bmr. GREEN (Officers Servant) Mil. Medal — all the foregoing for attending wounded under heavy shell fire on Sept. 17th — 1042 Driver Renvil (C/248 Batty) — for volunteering to convey orders under shell fire.	
		10.30 6.40 P.M.	Are off R.19.b-32×72 kept under fire 2 Batteries firing 760 rounds.	
		4.0 P.M.	In accordance with 49th Div. Arty. Operation Order 3/AX/62 supported attack by 15th Div. on trenches N.E. of SCHWABEN — 5" 18 Pdr. & 4.5" Hr. Battys. fired 1668 rounds. Attack successful.	
		10.P.M.	Div. on Night task (Blocking barrage) 3/18 Pdr. & 1 4.5" How. Baty. 400 rounds.	

HXS

Army Form C. 2118.

WAR DIARY
or
INTELLIGENCE SUMMARY

(Erase heading not required.)

Page 18

Place	Date	Hour	Summary of Events and Information	Remarks and references to Appendices
Centre Group Headquarters MESNIL (Q.34.J.10.95)	30.9.16	P.M. 11.15	Enemy shelled MESNIL Chateau and vicinity of these Headquarters with K.gas shells. Orders were received during the day for the relief of the 49th Div. Arty. the relief to be completed by 12.0 midday Oct 2nd by the 51st Div. Arty. This group except B/241 (45th Div.) Battery will be relieved by the 255th Brigade R.F.A.(T). B/241 Battery relieved to-day by C/85 Battery 18th Div. Arty.	MAPS As before

A.W.Stephenson

LIEUT. COL. R.F.A.,
COMDG. 248th. (W.R.) BRIGADE, R.F.A.

Army Form C. 2118.

WAR DIARY
or
INTELLIGENCE SUMMARY

(Erase heading not required.)

Instructions regarding War Diaries and Intelligence Summaries are contained in F. S. Regs., Part II. and the Staff Manual respectively. Title Pages will be prepared in manuscript.

Place	Date	Hour	Summary of Events and Information	Remarks and references to Appendices
			Vol 16 "War Diary 2 + 8th (U.R) Brigade R.F.A. from 1-10-1916 to 31-10-1916 Volume XV.	

2449 Wt. W14957/M90 750,000 1/16 J.B.C. & A. Forms/C.2118/12.

Army Form C. 2118.

WAR DIARY
or
INTELLIGENCE SUMMARY

(Erase heading not required.)

Page 1

Instructions regarding War Diaries and Intelligence Summaries are contained in F.S. Regs., Part II. and the Staff Manual respectively. Title Pages will be prepared in manuscript.

Place	Date	Hour	Summary of Events and Information	Remarks and references to Appendices
MESNIL – Centre Group Hqdqrs	1.10.16	10.30 A.M. to 4.0 P.M.	Areas R.19.6. 32.7.2. kept under continuous fire	MAP LENS 11 1/100,000
		4.0 P.M.	Carried out bombardment in support of attack by 18th Division – Attack successful	
		6.0 P.M.	Fired on French Right 2.6 R.19.6. 6.2.9.6 till 10.0 P.M.	
		8.0 P.M. 5.0 A.M.	Fired on defensive barrage line	
			Enemy shelled Q.28.D. twice during afternoon	
		11.15 P.M.	Enemy shelled MESNIL Valley heavily for two hours with K Gas shell which had been in progress for last two days completed	
HEDAUVILLE	2.10.16	12.0 midday	Relief by 51st Div. Arty.	
			Headquarters of 245th W.R. Bgde R.F.A. returned to Waggon Lines at HEDAUVILLE to which the Batteries of the Brigade had already returned. A very wet day.	
HE[?]GROUCHES	3.10.16	6.0 A.M.	Brigade marched to GROUCHES – 30 miles N.N.E. of DOULLENS – Another wet day	
SAULTY	4.10.16	11.0 A.M.	Brigade marched to SAULTY – 9 miles N.E. of DOULLENS	
	7.10.16		Batteries went into action under Group Commanders in the neighbourhood of BIENVILLERS–AU–BOIS – The Headquarters of the Brigade remained at SAULTY	
			No.2 being prepared for any Group	
	16.10.16		Orders received for the reorganisation of 49th Divnl. Artillery on basis of 3 Brigades with Six-gun Batteries instead of at present 4 Brigades with 4 Gun Batteries. The Scheme of reorganisation arranged to admit : – A/245 Battery joins 245th Brigade becoming C/245 – B/245 joins 246th Brigade becoming C/246 – Right Section C/245 joins 245 B Brigade – Left Section C/245 joins 246 B Brigade	
	18.10.16	11.30	Brigade marched to BUS–LES–ARTOIS where the reorganisation was carried out. The Headquarters of 245 Brigade went into billets at Bus and LOUVENCOURT Brigade Ammn. Column.	
ORVILLE	22.10.16		Headquarters 245 R.F.A. Brigade attached to 49th Divnl. Ammn. Col. at ORVILLE	

H.W. M[c]Pherson
LIEUT. COL. R.F.A.
COMDG. 245th (W.R) BRIGADE R.F.A.

121/6587

a 826

49th Division

4th W.R. Bde R.F.A.

Vol II

From 1- 31. 8. 15

Army Form C. 2118

WAR DIARY
or
INTELLIGENCE SUMMARY.
(Erase heading not required.)

CONFIDENTIAL

WAR DIARY

OF

4TH WEST RIDING (HOWITZER) BDE. R.F.A.

from 1-8-15 to 31-8-15

(VOLUME II)

Army Form C. 2118.

Page 17.

WAR DIARY
or
INTELLIGENCE SUMMARY.
(Erase heading not required)

Place	Date	Hour	Summary of Events and Information	Remarks and references to Appendices
ELVERDINGHE	1.8.15	11.15 a.m.	11th Battery fired 35 rounds on small wood E. of Railway C.1.d.2.3 and apparently silenced an enemy's Battery position. With apparently good effect. Enemy's artillery made active - intermittent bombardment of our trenches between FERME 14 and FORTIN 17 from 2.0 p.m. to 5.0 p.m. Intermittent shelling by enemy of trenches right of FORTIN 17 and behind French road trench on Left of FERME 14	Ref Sheet 28 N.W.
"	2.8.15			
"	3.8.15		At 11.45 a.m. Enemy sent 9 high Shrapnel (5.9) shells, 10 yards behind 10th Battery gun position - 7 more shells, 2 burst on gap. 10th Battery gun position. Enemy Shells BOESINGHE during the morning and TUGELA FARM intermittently throughout the day. 11th Battery fired 5 rounds at ammunition dump behind T at respect of G & C. 148th Inf. Bgde. At 12.0 noon 10th Battery fired 12 rounds at Trench Mortar reported by the one to the left of 7 which a Trench Mortar was reported to be particularly effective. 147th Infy Brigade - 3.9 close rounds were used. Trench Mortar. At 3.30 a.m. 11th Battery fired 2 rounds at A and B by M. 148th Infantry Bgde. located at about 1½ junction of A and B roads, with result of 1 round. The response satisfactory and 1 round of 1 round.	
"	5.8.15		At 2.45 p.m. 10th Battery (in conjunction with 9th M.T.B. (Heavy)) fired 17 rounds at farm at C.2.c.3.3 obtaining 3 direct hits	
"	6.8.15			

HKB Lt.

Army Form C. 2118.

Page 15

WAR DIARY
or
INTELLIGENCE SUMMARY.
(Erase heading not required.)

Place	Date	Hour	Summary of Events and Information	Remarks and references to Appendices
ELVERDINGHE	6.8.15		At 4.10 p.m. 11th & 63 Battery repeated yesterday's bombardment of Junction of Trenches 22, 23 and E	Ref. Map 28 N.W.
			C.7 d. 9.1.	
	7.8.15		In retaliation to fire of our Heavy Batteries Enemy during the night of 1a - 7a shelled the country road along our trenches inflicting only 1 casualty. 10th Battery had one casualty 5.9 and smaller shells (shrapnel) – 10th Battery had Gun position and bivouac heavily shelled – a shell entering a dugout at the Gun position and bursting inside killing one man – 5 other men + 4 horses followed up it fires. 10th Battery returned fire to be bombarded from points to be located	
		10 a.m.		
		11 a.m.	Battery registered our own communication trench to full extent of embrasures	
		6.30 p.m.	Battery registered our own communication trench when 63 Battery carried out pre-arranged programme of bombarding communicated Trenches to C.7.d. and hostile bombardment continued for an hour and three minutes	
	8.8.15		C.T.B. 2 hr bombardment during the night – above were fired during the night – 183 Rounds fired	
	9.8.15		A Quiet day - neither Batteries fired	
	10.8.15		Neither Battery fired - Some activity on part of Artillery on South of our front also bombing on our left	

WMG Col

Army Form C. 2118

Page 19.

WAR DIARY
or
INTELLIGENCE SUMMARY.
(Erase heading not required.)

Place	Date	Hour	Summary of Events and Information	Remarks and references to Appendices
Elverdinghe	11.8.15		Germans sent a good many "crumps" on L canal bank and fired 30 rounds at TUGELA FARM during morning - from 8 - 9 a.m. they shelled BOESINGHE and the house next to our O.P. At 11.30 a.m. the Germans shelled Brigade Headquarters Farm and continued till 12.45 by which time they had scored a number of direct hits and the building was almost demolished but there were no casualties.	
	12.8.15		Usual amount of crumping otherwise quiet day - neither Battery fired. Brigade Headquarters removed during night to three cottages close to ELVERDINGHE village.	
	13.8.15		A quiet day, neither Battery fired.	
	14.8.15		A good deal of heavy shelling in direction of Hamstring and Ypres by German heavy Batteries - 11th Battery fired 7 rounds at FERME 14 at request of 148th Infantry Brigade 1-3 rounds apparently effective. In the afternoon German shells heavily harassed points in the neighbourhood including PIONEER FARM next to old Brigade H.Q. billet which latter also received one shell. At 5.15 p.m. the 148th Infy Bgde reported massing of Germans at T and 11th Battery fired ten rounds near it the pioneers discovered it as supposed massing to be only an enemy working party taking planks and poles into trench. A considerable amount of new work done by enemy in his first trench at PIONEER'S GAP. At Report 2.14.5th Infy. 03gde, 11th Battery fired on French Howitzer left of FERME 14 with good result.	
"	15.8.15			H. W. S. Lee

WAR DIARY or INTELLIGENCE SUMMARY.

Army Form C. 2118.

Page 20.

Place	Date	Hour	Summary of Events and Information	Remarks and references to Appendices
ELVERDINGHE	16.8.15		Enemy shelled BOESINGHE at 12.25 p.m. A smoke shell and officer in Gun pit of Capt. Mostead at BOMBERS GAP 10th Battery at 12.30 p.m. fired 11 rounds at I Hypoed of 14B Infy. Brigade.	
	17.8.15		Intermittent shelling of BOESINGHE all day, also of ground in rear of our trenches — Enemy shelter BRIELEN and Batteries on neg. trenches in afternoon — At 4.0 p.m. 11th Battery fired 2 rounds at Redoubt and 2 at trench T. At 6.45 p.m. 10th Battery at request of 14B Infantry Brigade fired 6 rounds at Enemy trench mortar at ESSEN FARM. Considerable shelling by enemy in various directions including hard in front of 11th Battery and ELVERDINGHE and khervan at BOMBERS GAP and to C.R.A. Special report with sketch to be sent.	
"	18.8.15			
	19.8.15	10 am	A good deal of rifle fire heard during the night.	
	"	3.15 pm	The Germans shelled BOESINGHE with heavy shell. The trench 75.3 replied to german trench mortar whereupon Boches retaliated on our trenches with heavy shell. This has caused several times 9 officers to be sent with [signature]	

WAR DIARY
INTELLIGENCE SUMMARY.
(Erase heading not required.)

Army Form C. 2118

Page 21.

Instructions regarding War Diaries and Intelligence Summaries are contained in F. S. Regs., Part II. and the Staff Manual respectively. Title pages will be prepared in manuscript.

Place	Date	Hour	Summary of Events and Information	Remarks and references to Appendices
ELVERDINGHE	19.8.15.		the object of causing ill feeling between the English & French.	
"	"		The French fire intermittently on the area C8a 8.7.	
"	20.8.15.	4.5pm	During the night the germans shelled YSELKRANTZE Farm. A working party observed in infantry trenches at C8a 1.3 200 yds N of THATCHED COTTAGE was watched by 4th Siege By.	
"	"	6.10pm	118°F5 fired 3 rounds at FME 14 @ 3 at ITIEL COTT. in retaliation. Of 147th Hy Btle in retaliation.	
"	"	10.15pm	118°F5 fired 2 rounds at " " & 2 at MACKENSEN'S Farm for same purpose.	
"	"	10.40pm	Repeated above for same purpose.	
"	21.8.15	6.30	Four wooden structures in the form of wagon housing were observed on the PILKEM road at C8a 9.4½. Germans were observed signalling by coloured lights from C8a 2.1. following signals were seen. Two white " " 1 green	

WAR DIARY
or
INTELLIGENCE SUMMARY.
(Erase heading not required.)

Army Form C. 2118.

Page 22.

Place	Date	Hour	Summary of Events and Information	Remarks and references to Appendices
ELVERDINGHE.	22.8.	6.0 am	Both batteries fired a salute in conjunction with battery at a wedding party at C 8c 2.5½.	
"	23.8.		There was a bombardment by the French which drew the enemy's attention from our front during the day.	
"	24.8.		On behalf of the gunners in 5.9, fired a large number of which no less than 19 were put into BRIELEN area of which were seen. The activity amongst hostile aeroplanes.	
"	25.8.		A very quiet day.	
"	26.8.	6.5 pm	13th Bty fired 6 rounds a trench mortar at I. in retaliation at request of 146th Inf Bde.	
"	27.8.	9.30 am	Working parties observed at C7b 9½.2½ & at PILKEM C7b 1.1. Work being done at C7b 9½.2½ & at PILKEM.	
		7.37 pm	111th Bty retaliated in respect of 147th Inf & fired 2 rounds am. 7.	

[signature]

Army Form C. 2118.

Page 23.

WAR DIARY
or
INTELLIGENCE SUMMARY

(Erase heading not required.)

Place	Date	Hour	Summary of Events and Information	Remarks and references to Appendices
ELVERDINGHE	28.8.	—	German shells BOESINGHE between 1.30 & 2 p.m.	
"	29.8.	—	It very quiet day.	
"		11.45am.	10th Battery fired 20 rounds at a group at C.S.C.1.5.5. No direct hit was obtained but considerable damage was done to the trench done by. The light was bad to observation.	
"		11.50a.m.	fired 4 rounds at "T" (C.7.C.6.8) at group of 14 pr hy.	
"	30.8.	—	More artillery activity on both sides. Germans again relatively in our trenches in reply to French fire.	
"		2–4 p.m.	11th Battery fired a few on Farm 14. 3 times in retaliation of 148th hvy. R.S.	
"	31.8.	—	French artillery very active & the german reply was juicier than in the French front than hitherto.	
"		4.30	Farm at C7.C.3.2. was set on fire by french artillery. Some church of Ypres was observed from it.	

1577 Wt.W10791/1773 500,000 1/15 D.D. & L. A.D.S.S./Forms/C. 2118.

121/7016

49th Division

1/4 W.R. Bde R.F.A.

Vol III

Sept. 15

Army Form C. 2118

WAR DIARY
or
INTELLIGENCE SUMMARY.
(Erase heading not required.)

CONFIDENTIAL

WAR. DIARY
OF
4TH WEST RIDING (HOWITZER) B[DE], R.F.A.

From 1-9-15 to 30-9-15

(VOLUME III)

Instructions regarding War Diaries and Intelligence Summaries are contained in F. S. Regs., Part II. and the Staff Manual respectively. Title pages will be prepared in manuscript.

Place	Date	Hour	Summary of Events and Information	Remarks and references to Appendices

1577 Wt.W10791/1773 500,000 1/15 D. D. & L. A.D.S.S./Forms/C. 2118.

Army Form C. 2118

Page 1

WAR DIARY
or
INTELLIGENCE SUMMARY.
(Erase heading not required.)

Instructions regarding War Diaries and Intelligence Summaries are contained in F. S. Regs., Part II. and the Staff Manual respectively. Title pages will be prepared in manuscript.

Place	Date	Hour	Summary of Events and Information	Remarks and references to Appendices
Everdinghe ELVERDINGHE	1/9/15	3.42 p.m.	11th Battery at request of 148th Infantry Brigade fired 3 rds. at KIEL COTTAGE (C.7.d.6.6) and 2 rds. on T (C.7.c.6.8) - All the rounds were effective. Specially steep on T which silenced Enemy Trench Mortar immediately. Enemy shelled our Observation Station, killed Capt. R.T. Benn, 11th Battery & Major W. Denison and a Telephonist sent to Hospital suffering from shell shock.	References 2 maps B Series Sheet 28 N.W.
		4.15 p.m.		
"	2/9/15	3.0 p.m.	French Batteries shelled Enemy Trenches - Germans retaliated on CANAL BANK, BOESINGHE, VAALKATRANTZE, AEOLIAN and TUGELA FARMS and trenches in front.	
		3.30 p.m.	10th Battery registered Enemy Trench between TOOTH and TOOTHPICK Farms (C.7.B.10.4) firing 9 Rounds	
		4.40	11th Battery at request of 148th Infantry Bgde. fired at T (C.7.c.6.8) Enemy trench. Enemy retaliated	
		5.30	French Batteries repeated bombardment of Enemy trenches on CANAL BANK.	
"	3/9/15	3.0 p.m.	Duel between French and German Artillery	
		5.40	Enemy fired new form of Explosive - trail of white smoke left behind shell - a flame travelled direct to ground - smoke made by explosion very thick	
"	4/9/15	5.25 a.m.	Our 4.7 & Army German retaliated at 6.30 on CANAL BANK and AEOLIAN FARM	
		8.20 a.m.	French Artillery active - Hostile War Balloon up	
		8.40 a.m.	Smoke Balloon up, polish artillery again seen some piece (B.12.c)	
		5.30 p.m.	11th Battery fired 3 Rounds with good effect at T	

H.W. Stephenson
Lt. Col.

WAR DIARY or INTELLIGENCE SUMMARY

Army Form C. 2118.
Page 2

(Erase heading not required.)

Instructions regarding War Diaries and Intelligence Summaries are contained in F.S. Regs., Part II. and the Staff Manual respectively. Title pages will be prepared in manuscript.

Place	Date	Hour	Summary of Events and Information	Remarks and references to Appendices
ELVERDINGHE	5.9.15	1.3 p.m.	Our Heavy Artillery and Fread Battery very active – Germans retaliated	
		6.15	Enemy aeroplane flew over our lines rapidly by means of white lights.	
"	6.9.15	10.0 a.m.	Activity of enemy aeroplane which continued all day. 11th Battery report their buried telephone line to Observation Station cut in two places – evidently deliberately. Hostile Battery fired	
"	7.9.15	12.30	Enemy shelled the Farm at W (B.18.c.9.7) and our Observation Station on B.18.a.4.4.	
		1.30 p.m.	10th Battery registered KOLN FARM (C.14.B.8.6) firing 8 Rds.	
		3.45	11th Battery fired 3 effective Rounds at FERME 14 at present of 148th Inf Bgde.	
		4.20	Enemy Artillery and aircraft active throughout the day. Hostile Battery fired	
"	8.9.15		11th Battery fired 3 Rds. on FERME 14 by request of 148th Inf. Bgde.	
"	9.9.15	10.20 a.m.	Steps taken to find a new Observation Station. Hostile Battery shelled Reserve Trenches and Defence Works between B.23.c.7.8 and B.23.a.2.3 also BOESINGHE and CANAL BANK	
"	10.9.15	11.30 a.m. To 12.0 3.0 p.m.	10th Battery registered front trench at and W. of C.14.6.8.3 firing 30 rounds. 10th Battery registered HINDENBERG FARM firing 5 Rounds and obtaining 3 direct hits – Artillery both ends less active – our aircraft much in evidence	
"	11.9.15			
"	12.9.15	12.30 a.m.	11th Battery fired 4 Rds. at FERME 14 on Trench Mortar then at present of 148th Inf Bgde. New O.P. established at B.17.B.7.3½	

H.W.A. Thomson
Lt. Col.

WAR DIARY
or
INTELLIGENCE SUMMARY.
(Erase heading not required.)

Army Form C. 2118.
Page 3

Place	Date	Hour	Summary of Events and Information	Remarks and references to Appendices
ELVERDINGHE	13.9.15	8 a.m.	German Artillery Active - Shelled road from BRIELEN B.29.a.2.4 and Bridge B.22.d.5.9 first with H.E. and then with Gas Shell	
		9 a.m.	B.22.d.5.9 first with H.E. and then with Gas Shell	
			10th W.R. Battery fired 18 Rds. Registration at point C.14.b.2.5. and C.14.b.9. 3 hostile aeroplanes	
		11 a.m.	observation — much delay by activity of enemy aeroplanes	
		1.10 p.m.	Our Heavy Artillery shelled Trenches in front of AEOLIAN FARM	
		6.15 p.m.	BRIELEN - ELVERDINGHE Road shelled for about an hour also 11th Battery billets where the Gunners are. 11th Battery report that they located this shelling is due to the fact that the traffic on this road can be seen from Enemy Balloon and that he has attacked	
"	14.9.15 4-4½ p.m.		Enemy shelled MODDER FARM (B.17.d.8.5) for two hours obtaining 20 direct hits. Gen Enemy Balloon up during day Exceptionally quiet day, neither Battery fired	
"	15.9.15		Exceptionally quiet day, neither Battery fired	
"	16.9.15 6 p.m.		Enemy Shelled MODDER FARM (B.13.d.8.5) - otherwise day very quiet till evening when Enemy at 6.0 p.m. and 8.0 p.m. Shelled Road & an Farm behind Battery positions.	
"	17.9.15 11 a.m.		Enemy fired 2 searching shells pooh? which went into an?? observed	
			Enemy Artillery active all day ELVERDINGHE village an Road thence to BRIELEN Shelled persistently all afternoon	
	4.9 p.m.		10th Battery fired 9 Rds. in Registration of C.14.b.8.9 (aeroplane observation)	
	5 p.m.		10th Battery fired 6 Rds. at payment of infantry a Trench in front of E.24. 10th Battery fired 10 Rds (Shrapnel) at an Enemy shelled O.P.	
"	18.9.15		ELVERDINGHE shelled at intervals throughout the day - shells (shrapnel) fell in front of 10th Battery Position about 4.45 p.m. 11th Battery shelled during afternoon at C.2.C.4.3 during afternoon	

H.N.A.Thomson
Br. Cdr.

Army Form C. 2118

WAR DIARY
or
INTELLIGENCE SUMMARY.
(Erase heading not required).

Instructions regarding War Diaries and Intelligence Summaries are contained in F.S. Regs., Part II. and the Staff Manual respectively. Title pages will be prepared in manuscript.

Place	Date	Hour	Summary of Events and Information	Remarks and references to Appendices
BRIELEN	23 Sept	12 mid night to 6pm	The Day was quiet and there was little hostile shelling. Haze apparently kept the hostile Observation Balloons down. Rounds fired – NIL.	Reference Map B Sector Sheet 28 N.W. HSD
"	23	6pm to 6pm	The Day was very quiet and observation difficult owing to mist. Little enemy shelling in our area. Rounds fired – NIL.	HSD
"	24	6pm to 6pm	Worked portion of night & all day on position & Dugouts. 6.30 pm Flash of gun (probably 5.9) observed 37½° magnetic from LEIPSIG FARM. B.23.c.5.3 (28 N.W. BELGIUM) firing into woods in II.6.6. 5.30am to 6.30am. In accordance with Operation Orders bombarded points behind line in zone as follows. MG emplacements at C.14.a 5.7 & C.14.a 8.5 & French tramway running from HINDENBURG FARM C.8.d.10.2 to 5 CHEMINS ESTAMINET. C.14.a.8.8 (all Reference map BOESINGHE I/10000) Rounds fired – 99 –	
"	25	6pm to 6pm	6.30 am. As Centre Group ceased firing the BAKERY in BRIELEN stoked up a thick yellow column of smoke, very visible, was the nearest at 6.34 not a vestige of smoke remained. Reports to Group Commander (Lieut Col. E.B. Whiteley) by telephone received orders to watch it & report if it happened again as a suspicious mile. Aeroplane scout instructed.	HSD
"	25	6pm to 6pm	Very quiet day & night. 4.30 pm Heavy Howitzer (17 inch?) fired 2 rounds towards VLAMERTINGHE.	
"	26	6pm to 6pm	5.15 pm 15.520h. Two aeroplanes of unknown but suspected Boche make manoeuvred very low over trenches held by 146th Inf. Bde. One dropped 2 light signals (afterwards heard that one was French) was compelled to alight behind HINDENBURG FARM, the pilot being wounded) Observer battered up this afternoon. Magnetic bearing from WELL COTTAGE. B.22.d.7.8½. 99° Rounds fired – NIL	HSD

Army Form C. 2118

WAR DIARY
or
INTELLIGENCE SUMMARY.
(Erase heading not required.)

Instructions regarding War Diaries and Intelligence Summaries are contained in F. S. Regs., Part II and the Staff Manual respectively. Title pages will be prepared in manuscript.

Place	Date	Hour	Summary of Events and Information	Remarks and references to Appendices
BRIELEN	26th to 27	5.30 p	Nothing to report. Worked on Dug outs on position. Rounds fired - NIL.	HSD
"	27. to 28	5.30 p — 5.30	9.17.am Group Retaliation Order. 9.20. Fired 1 Salvo. 9.39 Group Retaliation Order on D21 D22. Fired 1 Salvo. 9.45. Fired 10 Rounds at request of GOC Right Infantry Brigade. on enemy trenches from C14 a 9.1 to C 14 b 5 4. 10 am Group Retaliation Order. 10.1. Fired 1 Salvo. 10.7. Orders received from Group Commander to fire 8 rounds on VON KLUCKS COTTAGE (C14 b.3.2½) KRUPP FARM (C14 a.9.1) & ESSEN FARM (C.14 a 8 2½). 10.14. Rounds fired. 10.30. Orders received from Group Commander to fire 12 Rounds on same 3 points. 10.34. Rounds fired. 10.47. Orders received to Cease Fire. Rounds fired - 42.	HSD
	27th to 28th	5.30 p — 5:30	Nothing to report. Rounds fired - NIL.	HSD

WAR DIARY
or
INTELLIGENCE SUMMARY.
(Erase heading not required.)

Army Form C. 2118

Place	Date	Hour	Summary of Events and Information	Remarks and references to Appendices
BRIELEN	29th to 30th	5.30 a.m.	3.15. Hostile 5.9 Battery put 8 HE shell in air in the vicinity of LEIPSIC FARM. B23 c.5.3 Fuze marked Dopp.Z c/92.St.Set 21°.15″. No damage.	
		5.30	Also found round brass hollow cap Nyt d3E. Threaded inside. 1½″ in diameter. Painted scarlet. marked. HZ. 05 G. St 15 M.	HSD
			Rounds fired — NIL.	

WAR DIARY
or
INTELLIGENCE SUMMARY.
(Erase heading not required.)

Army Form C. 2118
Page 4

Place	Date	Hour	Summary of Events and Information	Remarks and references to Appendices
ELVERDINGHE	19.9.15	9.30 a.m. 10.30 a.m. 2.30 p.m.	Horse in front of 10th Battery and defence works adjacent shelled with 5.9 H.E. ELVERDINGHE — BRIELEN Road (behind Battery Gun Position) shelled with P. Shrap & H.E. about 20 or 30 rounds being fired. 11th Battery Report that in Pilckem day about 1½ & 2.8½ Gun Aircraft was on Enemy O.P. Return up near PILCKEM all day. German Aeroplane dropped white lights over position in front of Battery on the Enemy Aeroplane.	
	20.9. & 6.15 th.		ELVERDINGHE — BRIELEN Rd (B.15.d.2.3.) Which had been immediately shelled with H.E. 5.9 shell.	
	20.9.15	7.00 a.m.	Position in front of Brewery again shelled with 5.9 H.E. Position in front of Battery shelled numerous positions in Enemy Battery very active all day. BRIELEN — BOESINGHE also neighbourhood of ELVERDINGHE and BRIELEN — POPERINGHE shelled during afternoon. Ammunition Col. Report HOUTHULST FOREST area shelled — Enemy Aircraft acted over Allies active raid on HOUTHULST FOREST area. For the first time once Allies active all day. Hostile aircraft active all day.	
	21.9.15	7.00 p.m.	ELVERDINGHE shelled with 5.9 H.E. — lived in front of 10th Battery position here. Enemy artillery active all day — lived in front of 10th Battery position here. Enemy artillery fire just moderately heavy in Southerly direction. Shelled — Enemy artillery fire ELVERDINGHE shelled on morning & 10.5.	
	22.9.15		Enemy artillery active all day. ELVERDINGHE shells a partly damaged — many other positions. Billets, officers shelled own partly damaged.	
	40 1 m.		shells bombarded following points C.8.d.10.3, C.14.a.9.9, C.14.&.5.9. 10th Battery: " " C.14.b.8.5, C.14.a.4.10 and C.14.a.5.6. 11th " " 11th Battery: Report they shelled O.P. at C.21.a.4.3 and between the frank & H.W.Cameron Capt.	

WAR DIARY
or
INTELLIGENCE SUMMARY.

(Erase heading not required.)

Army Form C. 2118.

Place	Date	Hour	Summary of Events and Information	Remarks and references to Appendices
ELVERDINGHE	30.9.15		A quiet day - 10th W.R. Battery report that at 6.0 a.m. Enemy shelled old Battery position at B.29.b.2.6. 8 Rounds of 5.9 H.E. being fired. 10th Battery report hostile balloon up at 4.30 p.m. Magnetic bearing 67° from B.23.b.5.3 Hostile aeroplanes got well over lines and checked by Anti-aircraft gun fire in the evening about 8-30	

W.H.Stephenson
LIEUT. COL. R.F.A.
COMDG. 4TH W.R. (HOWZR.) BDE. R.F.A.

WAR DIARY
or
INTELLIGENCE SUMMARY

CONFIDENTIAL

WAR DIARY

OF

10ᵗʰ W.R. (HOW) BTY

4ᵀᴴ WEST RIDING (HOWITZER) Bᴰᴱ, R.F.A.

From 23-9-15 to 29-9-15

(VOLUME I)

Army Form C. 2118

WAR DIARY
or
INTELLIGENCE SUMMARY.
(Erase heading not required.)

CONFIDENTIAL

WAR DIARY

OF

11th W.R. (How.) Bty

4TH WEST RIDING (HOWITZER) BDE, R.F.A.

From 23.9.15   To 29.9.15

(VOLUME I)

Army Form C. 2118

WAR DIARY
or
INTELLIGENCE SUMMARY.
(Erase heading not required.)

Instructions regarding War Diaries and Intelligence Summaries are contained in F. S. Regs., Part II. and the Staff Manual respectively. Title pages will be prepared in manuscript.

Place	Date	Hour	Summary of Events and Information	Remarks and references to Appendices
BRIELEN	23.9.15	9.30 A.M.	Hostile aeroplane was active along the line in Square C. (Ref. 2nd Army Sheet I 1/40,000.) but was driven off by our A.A. Guns.	P.C.P.
do.	do.	7.0 P.M.	On the whole the enemy was less active on the immediate front 15-day. About 6 hostile shrapnel shells fell about B.29.a.0.6. Weather conditions good. Three to four heavy shells were heard travelling towards YPRES.	
do.	24.9.15	9.30 P.M.	Hostile shelling BRIELEN with approx 5.9" How. These shells fell chiefly in the neighbourhood of the Church.	P.C.P.
do.	do.	11.30 A.M. to 12.30 P.M.	Enemy aircraft not active to-day, probably due to inclement weather.	
do.	25.9.15	6.30 A.M.	The battery fired on the following points:- C.8.C.12, EOLIAN FARM (C.26.25), C.7.d.5.8, C.7 central, MACKENSEN FARM (C.B.c.5.7), OSCAR FARM (C.8.a.6.3), and C.7.b.5.3 with effect. One hundred rounds were fired in all. The enemy were not expected to a smoke attack from our own front trenches during this period the following is a report on its operations:- At 5.56 A.M. Smoke appeared. It emitted most satisfactorily keeping almost horizontal and very dense during progress to hostile trench. The pace of the wind (approx 8 miles per hr) seemed most suitable for smoke of this density. The clouds seemed to diffuse to height of about 200 ft. and dispersed within twenty as thirty minutes upon being turned off. The first point was very statickly standard in right field at this time 15 twenty's front direct suggesting that this was very badly felt at this time - so there were the enemy held a return that claimed to be a considerable number on his parapet for Kruck, suggesting by rifle fire. The enemy shelled (B.18.a.4.3) and HULLS FARM Trenches and WAGON PARK (B.18.a.4.3) and HULLS FARM (B.18.C.8.3 with gas shells.	

WAR DIARY
or
INTELLIGENCE SUMMARY.

(Erase heading not required.)

Army Form C. 2118

Instructions regarding War Diaries and Intelligence Summaries are contained in F. S. Regs., Part II. and the Staff Manual respectively. Title pages will be prepared in manuscript.

Place	Date	Hour	Summary of Events and Information	Remarks and references to Appendices
BRIELEN	25.9.15	5.15 A.M.	Heavy gun heard firing from well to the rear of PILCKEM in direction of YPRES	Ref: Moore 2nd Army Sect.
do.	do.	7.15 A.M.	Hostile Planes active and Hostile Balloon up E.N.E. of BRIELEN.	
do.	do.	7.25 A.M.	At request of 146 Inf. Bde. Ist battery opened + Ruth on C.7. d.5.8 and C.7.d.5.6. Fire was witheld for 5 minutes on account of the Shutter not yet having cleared?	P.C.?
do.	26.9.15	11.45 A.M.	Hostile Plane patrolling front line but went back by on A.A. guns	
do.	do.	2.30 p.m.	PILCKEM Balloon are up. i.e. Balloon N.E. of BRIELEN + two near a "quicker" bay on Houthulst Histerning? seemed somewhat subdued. The weather was warm but cloudy	P.C.?
do.	do.	4.25 p.m.	Heavy shell heard falling near VLAMERTINGHE and hostile Balloon up E.N.E. of BRIELEN	
do.	do.	4.14 p.m.	" " " "	
do.	do.	5.18 p.m.	" " " "	
do.	do.	5.18 p.m.	One of our aeroplanes was brought down about C.B. 50° from B.28.6.7.10. Balloon was up bw. E. of BRIELEN & hostile aircraft active	P.C.P.
do.	27.9.15	10.40 p.m.	Replies were fired from B.28.c.7.9. @ C.B. 40 and C.13. 50°	
do.	28.9.15	7.56 A.M.	Nothing of any note observed. 16. Jay? & hostile shrap reported	
do.	do.	8.10 A.M.	Two heavy? shells fell near VLAMERTINGHE	
do.	do.	9.18 A.M.	At request of 146 Inf. Bde. 3 rounds were fired on Trenches at C.7.c.5.8. and C.7.d.5.6.	9 Rounds fr'm 9.25 A.M.
do.	do.	9.30 A.M.	German balloon up due S. of BRIELEN.	
do.	29.9.15	8.50 A.M.	German Balloon up C.A. 84° from B.28.6.7.9.	
do.	do.	2.50 p.m.	After hostile shrapnel fell about Dawson's CORNER B.23.c.87 also some crumps about B.23.c.86. otherwise a very quiet day, hostile arty.	P.C.

1577 Wt. W10791/1773 50,000 1/15 D. D. & L. A.D.S.S./Forms/C. 2118.

49th Division

4th W. R. Bde RFA

Vol IV

Oct 15

Army Form C. 2118.

WAR DIARY
or
INTELLIGENCE SUMMARY.
(Erase heading not required.)

Instructions regarding War Diaries and Intelligence Summaries are contained in F. S. Regs., Part II. and the Staff Manual respectively. Title pages will be prepared in manuscript.

Place	Date	Hour	Summary of Events and Information	Remarks and references to Appendices

CONFIDENTIAL

WAR DIARY

OF

4TH WEST RIDING (HOWITZER) BDE. R.F.A.

From 1-10-15 to 31.10.15.

(VOLUME IX)

Army Form C. 2118.
Page 1

WAR DIARY
or
INTELLIGENCE SUMMARY.
(Erase heading not required.)

Instructions regarding War Diaries and Intelligence Summaries are contained in F. S. Regs., Part II. and the Staff Manual respectively. Title pages will be prepared in manuscript.

Place	Date	Hour	Summary of Events and Information	Remarks and references to Appendices
ELVERDINGHE	1.10.15	8.0 a.m.	10th W. R. Battery fired, at request of 147th Infy. Brigade, 12 rounds in retaliation on German front trench between C.14.b.9.3 and E.14.a.9.1 (searching) — 147th Infy. Brigade subsequently reported on the shooting as follows:— "Result of your shooting this morning — Parapet knocked down in one or two places — several direct hits — shooting looked good."	BELGIUM (B SERIES) SHEET 28 N.W.
		1.15 1.45 6 p.m.	Enemy shelled MALAKOFF FARM (B.21.b.2.0) and REDAN FARM (B.22.a.2.8) and DAWSON'S CORNER (B.22.c.5.5) with H.E. and shrapnel. Enemy shelled BRIELEN – ELVERDINGHE Road with 5.9 H.E.	
		3.30 p.m.	Enemy shelled Battery front – 2 Hostile Observation Balloons up.	
	2.10.15 3.10.15		A quiet day — neither Battery fired — Another quiet day.	
	4.10.15		Enemy Artillery more active – 10th Battery report that at 4.15 p.m. Enemy shelled B.28.c.8.5 – High velocity guns being used of apparently 5.2 calibre magnetic bearing 40° from B.23.c.5.4. 11th Battery report appearance of seven at C.1.a.5.5 manned presumably — reported at C.R.A. and C.R.L.	
	6.8.63 a.m. 6.		10th Battery received message from C.R.A. (through H.Q.Sp.) to retaliate on in front of F.21 – Fired at 6.11 a.m. 12 rounds – The 148th Infy Brigade reported shooting very fine an effective. Both Batteries in accordance with orders made a single fine each selected positions and registered various points in their respective zone with their Guns – Hostile Balloons up all day.	

AMS

WAR DIARY
or
INTELLIGENCE SUMMARY.
(Erase heading not required)

Army Form C. 2118.
Page 2

Place	Date	Hour	Summary of Events and Information	Remarks and references to Appendices
ELVERDINGHE	5.10.15	6.52 a.m.	10th Battery received calls from 148th Infy. Brigade to retaliate on Enemy trenches opposite E.23.24 and 2.5 - Fired 11 Rounds	
		7.12	10th Battery received further similar calls - Fired 8 Rounds. Both Batteries fired on various points with their clinometer angle guns during day. Enemy's artillery active all day.	
	6.10.15		A very quiet day - Both Batteries withdrew their detached guns during day in conformity with orders received from C.R.A.	
	7.10.15	12.0 noon	Enemy shelled BRIELEN—ELVERDINGHE ROAD and avenue leading to CHATEAU de TROIS TOURS - Hostile Balloon up over PILCKEM The Corps Commander visited the 4th W.R. Bgde. Ammn. Col. and inspected his cata factor, with condition of horses and horse Camp generally.	
	8.10.15		A misty day - no artillery activity - The Division Commander visited Bgde. Head Quarter and went round the Batteries in the afternoon	
	9.10.15		Another misty day - No artillery activity - Nothing doing	
	10.10.15		A clear day - Enemy Aircraft and Artillery more active and hostile aeroplane over the Enemy aircraft and our artillery active - (a high velocity Battery [Battery position] fired 2 Rounds Shrapnel behind LEIPSIG FARM (10th Battery position) and then 9 rounds to shell BRIELEN	
	11.10.15	3.30 4 pm	10th Battery fired during the night (10.o/11.a) at 10.45 p.m. at request of 148th Infy. Bgde. 8 Rounds on C.14.B.8.8 and C.14.B.8.5.2. Hostile Biplane was apparently hit by a 2Pdr. Q.F. Gun at 11.5 a.m. while flying between BRIELEN and YPRES.	

HWA

Army Form C. 2118.

Page 3

WAR DIARY
or
INTELLIGENCE SUMMARY.
(Erase heading not required.)

Instructions regarding War Diaries and Intelligence Summaries are contained in F. S. Regs., Part II. and the Staff Manual respectively. Title pages will be prepared in manuscript.

Place	Date	Hour	Summary of Events and Information	Remarks and references to Appendices
ELVERDINGHE	12.10.15	6.45 A.M.	10th W.R. Battery fired 14 rounds on HIGH COMMAND REDOUBT (C.14.b.2.5) at the request of G.O.C. 148th Infy Brigade	
		3.30 P.M.	ELVERDINGHE shelled and again at 5.30 P.M.	
		5.30 P.M.	Hostile Aeroplane over Battery positions - Balloon (Enemy) up all day.	
	13.10.15	12.0 P.M.	An aeroplane with orders from C.R.A. 10th Battery methodically bombarded KRUPP FARM (C.14.a.9.1) and Enemy Trenches (New) from that point to HIGH COMMAND REDOUBT and Rear trenches from C.14.b.2.5 to C.14.b.8.2.5 firing 40 rounds on F.O.O reports trees much out of stay Enemy trenches being severely damaged and several direct hits being obtained on HIGH COMMAND REDOUBT	
			11th Battery bombarded Communication trenches C.7.d.9.2 to C.8.c.1.2 MACKENSEN FARM and C.7.d.8.5 to EOLIAN FARM	
			F.O.O reported detonation in a very farm	
		5.15 P.M.	Enemy shelled ELVERDINGHE and BRIELEN	
		6.30 P.M.	Enemy retaliated for afternoon bombardment by shelling all our O.P's which transport and Infantry reliefs were proceeded another country side severely	
		10.30 P.M.	11th Battery retaliated firing 20 rounds on KIEL COTTAGE MAUSER COTTAGE	
		9.55 p.m.	EOLIAN FARM and trench C.8.c.1.2	
	14.10.15		a quiet day	
	15.10.15		L.F.Bg day and very quiet - G.O.C. R.A (in-ents of Col 73 attached	
	16.10.15	7.57 A.M.	148th Infy Brigade called on 10th Battery to retaliate on C.14.b.6.2 and C.14.a.3.5 similar order later by C.R.A fired 24 Rds. Ceased firing 2.20 p.m.	
		2.10 P.M.	Left Infy Brigade called on 11th Battery to retaliate - 8 Rds fired on FERM E14 and 7(C.7.c.7.9)	
		2.35 P.M.	11th Battery again called up on 12 Rds on EOLIAN FARM (C.8.c.2.5) and KIEL COTTAGE (C.7.d.5.6) 2.50 P.M. a further 12 rounds fired on EOLIAN FARM.	

AMD

WAR DIARY or INTELLIGENCE SUMMARY

Army Form C. 2118.

Page 4

Places	Date	Hour	Summary of Events and Information	Remarks and references to Appendices
ELVERDINGHE (contd)	16.10.15	2.15 PM	10th Battery received report from 148th Infy. Bgde. that enemy were collecting in Sap opposite E.29 and fired 8 rounds at their parapet in the front	
	17.10.15		A misty day, but clear of aeroplanes in afternoon during which there was some artillery activity. Otherwise a quiet day.	
	18.10.15		A fairly quiet day – 10th WR Battery at 2.58 p.m. fired 9 rounds retaliation on ESSEN FARM (C.14.d.7.25) at request of Right (148th) Infantry Brigade	
	19.10.15		A fine clear day with considerable artillery and aerial activity	
		1.23 p.m.	10th WR Battery requested by 148th (Right) Infantry Brigade to retaliate on enemy parapet opposite E.24 – E.25 and fired 10 rounds	
		1.52	Repeat repeated – 10 more rounds fired	
		2.20	Further retaliation requested on enemy front trench at C.14.B.2.5 — 10 rounds fired	
		4.20	11th W.R. Battery ordered by C.R.A. to fire 12 Rounds at Enemy Trench running from C.7.d.9.1 E. and then S.E. Issued B5 KOLN FARM.	
		5-5	Batn. Battery orders by C.R.A. to fire 12 Rds. on enemy front trench C.7.d.5.6 to C.7.d.9.1	
		5-10	10th W.R. Battery ordered by C.R.A. to shell trenches from C.8.C.1.2 to C.14.a. 3.5 — fired 12 Rds.	
			148th Infty. Brigade reported obstinate Boo? A quieter day – neither Battery was called upon to fire	
	20.10.15			
	21.10.15	7.25 a.m.	10th W.R. Battery in accordance with orders from C.R.A. fired 20 rounds on enemy trenches from C.14.a.1.9 to C.14.a.5.5	
		10.35 a.m.	Similar report received from 148th Infy. Bgde. – 20 rounds fired	
		1.30 p.m.	At request of 148 Infy Bgde. 10th Battery fires 8 rounds in enemy parapet C.14 B.3.5	
		8.5 p.m.	148th Infy. Bgde. requested 10th Battery to fire retaliation against head of C.14 B.5.3 and 11th COMMAND REDOUBT C.14.B.9.3 – 8 Rounds fired	
		7.46 a.m.	11th Battery by orders of C.R.A. fired 12 Rds. on trench running from C.8.c.9.1 to KIEL COT. (C.7.d.5.6) Shooting reported effective by infantry	

Army Form C. 2118.
Page 5

WAR DIARY
or
INTELLIGENCE SUMMARY.
(Erase heading not required.)

Instructions regarding War Diaries and Intelligence Summaries are contained in F. S. Regs., Part II. and the Staff Manual respectively. Title pages will be prepared in manuscript.

Place	Date	Hour	Summary of Events and Information	Remarks and references to Appendices
ELVERDINGHE	22.10.15	12.35 P.M.	11th W.R. Battery fired 6 rounds at FERME 14 to prepare a 147th Infy. Brigade	
		10.45	" 2 " " T (C.7.c.8.9)	
		12.50	" " " some fresh earth on C.7.6.5.5 and C.7.6.9.5 by C.R.A's orders	
		1.54	" " " some fresh earth on " " " with 40 lb shell	
			During the afternoon the Battery registered aiming point with the new 40 lb shell (which is expected to fire the Sectanber new range of 1400yds) with fairly satisfactory results. A good deal of General Artillery and aerial activity — fine day.	
	23.10.15		10th Battery tried to register with 40lb shell but light insufficient. A misty day — 10th Battery tried to register with 40 lb shell but light insufficient.	
	24.10.15		During night 23/24 Enemy shelled ELVERDINGHE, BRIELEN, VLAMERTINGHE, POPERINGHE, DAWSONS CORNER &c. But the whole countryside behind the infantry trenches — S.W. end of ELVERDINGHE practically deluged in fumes — little Battery fire.	
	25.10.15		Misty day — very quiet — hostile Battery fire	
	26.10.15		Bright day — Enemy Artillery and aircraft active — Hostile balloon up — 10th Battery carried out registration with 40 lb shell	
	27.10.15		H.M. King inspected on ABEELE aviation ground 3 composite Battalions representing respectively 2 Division composing 6th Corps — Artillery of 49th Div. found an Company O.R. and 15 N.C.O.s and men represented this Brigade. A wet day not much activity	
	28.10.15		A very wet day. G.O.C. R.A. carried both Batteries. Enemy high velocity fire. from the side of Oaliens fire on 6 Shell about B.25.C.	
	29.10.15		Enemy artillery fire intermittently — neither battery fired.	
	30.10.15		A dull day. No aerial activity.	
			A good deal of hostile shelling and aeroplane activity of an intermittent character. The 11th Battery did some registration with 40lb shell and aeroplane observation difficult had to desist owing to the haze making observation difficult	
	31.10.15		A little hostile shelling in the morning in the direction of the Canal Bank and VLAMERTINGHE, otherwise the day was quiet — some rain in the afternoon, neither Battery fired	

H.W. Litheren
Lieut. Col. R.F.A.
Comdg. 4th W. R. (Howzr.) Bde. R.F.A.

1577 Wt. W10791/1773 500,000 1/15 D. D. & L. A.D.S.S./Form/C. 2118.

Army Form C. 2118

WAR DIARY
or
INTELLIGENCE SUMMARY.
(Erase heading not required.)

CONFIDENTIAL.

WAR DIARY

OF

1/4TH WEST RIDING (HOWITZER) BDE, R.F.A.

from 1-11-15 to 30-11-15

(VOLUME V)

WAR DIARY or INTELLIGENCE SUMMARY

Army Form C. 2118

Page 1

Place	Date	Hour	Summary of Events and Information	Remarks and references to Appendices
ELVERDINGHE	1.11.15		A wet day - neither Battery fired but enemy artillery fairly active shelling during the day MODDER FARM and Map B.23.a, BRIELEN & villages N of the (Canal Bank to the N. Two officers joined ADVTG wounded on 7 days another wet day - neither Battery fired - Enemy artillery on active. Enemy artillery	MAP BELGIUM (B Series) Sheet 28 N.W.
	2.11.15			
	3.11.15		A fine day - Both Batteries did some registration with 40 lb shell - Enemy artillery active and shelled many points during the day including ELVERDINGHE, BOESINGHE (39 H.E. 5"9 Shells) DAWSON'S CORNER (B.22. c.8. 7%)(40 How. 4.2" shells)	
	4.11.15		A wet morning fine later - neither Battery fired - Enemy artillery again active - Neighbourhood of DAWSON'S CORNER - N.W. of d (B.20.b.) came in for much attention - being shelled no fewer than five times during the day with a total number of 76 (How) 4.2 Shells	
	5.11.15		Large shell were heard going in the direction of YPRES A day of great artillery activity on both sides - Enemy trenches reported flooded and many of their working parties out drawing and repairing them. C.R.A. therefor ordered all Batteries to fire intermittently by day and night on certain points. Enemy artillery also very active shelled many places including ELVERDINGHE VILLAGE and Road thence to BRIELEN, the latter village, PIONEER FARM and MODDERFARM - Our trenches also constantly shelled. 112th Battery registered OSCAR FARM (C.8.A.6.2) with 40 lb Shell	
	6.11.15		Artillery on both sides again active - Both Batteries shelled intermittently the Enemys trenches in order the prevent repair - Enemy shelled ELVERDINGHE heavily with guns of various calibre at 12.30 p.m. BRIELEN also shelled	
	7.11.15		Artillery active - Both Batteries continue intermittent fire in front in aid of by C.R.A. In addition 110 Battery registered two targets not to 110 C.R.A. In enemy trenches shell and aeroplane observation - also fired on German battery indicated by aeroplane	
		1.57 p.m.	112th Battery fired 12 rounds on "T" (C.7.C.6.8) at request of 147th Infantry Brigade.	HMcL

Army Form C. 2118

Page 2

WAR DIARY
or
INTELLIGENCE SUMMARY.
(Erase heading not required.)

Place	Date	Hour	Summary of Events and Information	Remarks and references to Appendices
ELVERDINGHE	8.11.15	12.45 P.M.	Artillery active - Enemy shelled most of their favourite targets (DAWSONS CORNER twice) and also our trenches.	
		2.33	10th Battery fired 12 rounds in retaliation on enemy front trench at C.14.b.4.2½ at request of 8th W. YORKS. Regt.	
		3.25	Same Battery a similar response - fired 4 rounds on C.14.b.7.3	
			Same Battery on similar request fired 6 rounds on enemy pear trench C.14.b.8.6 & C.14.b.5.5. Infantry reported shooting good - 1 direct hit on front trenches - Reported hostile observation.	
			11th Battery fired on points indicated by C.R.A. as before.	
	9.11.15		Artillery both sides active. Enemy shelled most of their usual targets.	
		10.20 A.M.	10th OB Battery at request of 5th W. YORKS. Regt. retaliated on enemy front trench at C.14.b.9.3 and C.14.b.7.3 and swept rear trench - fired 24 rounds. (Hostile shelling ceased)	
		1.53 P.M.	At request of G.O.C. 148th Infantry Bde. 10th Batty. fired 4 rounds on trench mortar at C14.A.8.5	
		2.20 P.M.	A pullin up pound fired d indicated by C.R.A. - A very noisy day.	
			Both Batteries fired at intervals on points indicated by C.R.A.	
	10.11.15		A good deal of hostile shelling.	
		10 A	Battery fired occasional rounds on hurrying orders by C.R.A.	
		11 A	Battery fired 12 occasional rounds and also by official order of C.R.A. 30 rounds Battery trenches C.7.d.6.6, C.7.d.5.6 to C.7.d.4.5	
		12.57 P.M.	Enemy Artillery very active - all day shelling the Brigade area of Guerre (B.20.b.d.W.)	
			Enemy Artillery very active. all day shelling the Brigade and Gun Road (Barkin School) and Gun Road (B.20.b.d.w.) BOEIL (PEULISSIER FARM) GRENADIER FARM (Bandhen School) and Gun Road B.21.a.c.) - Rest of Batteries fired occasional rounds as before.	
	11.11.15	2.30 P.M.	10 A Battery fired 9 rounds (3 salvoes of 3 Guns) on enemy Trench Mortars behind HIGH COMMAND REDOUBT at request of G.O.C. 148th Infantry Brigade.	
			Enemy Baloon up all day.	

HKS

WAR DIARY
or
INTELLIGENCE SUMMARY.

Army Form C. 2118

Page 3

Place	Date	Hour	Summary of Events and Information	Remarks and references to Appendices
ELVERDINGHE	12.11.15		A very quiet day — Bath Batteries shot intermittently on special tasks	
	13.11.15		A stormy day — Enemy Artillery quiet — Batteries had occasional finds a tasks	
	14.11.15		A very clear fine day. Enemy Artillery active on many targets behind our trenches. Shelling CANAL BANK, BRIELEN, CHATEAU TROIS TOURS, VLAMERTINGHE with all calibres up to 8". Battery at "B" in Central Enemy an exchange — Batteries of retaliating on the 4.7 Battery and B.M. Battery active. Bath Batteries registered target point and approach Enemy Artillery again active on Cogge at 3.0 p.m. first Balloon within their perspective zones in the morning and again at 3 p.m.	
	15.11.15		A same kind on part of Artillery demonstration in accordance with Divisional orders. In addition 10th Battery retaliated to the shelling of our Engineer Dumps at N°4 Canal Bank by shelling Enemy Dump at C.9.d.2.7 by request of 146th Infy Brigade. Enemy Balloon up. Enemy Artillery active. C10 "G" Battery kept Enemy retaliation at regiment 146 H. Infy (C.15.d.7.8) Brigade on HIGH COMMAND REDOUBT, HINDENBERG-FARM (C.8.d.10.2) VON SPEE FARM (C.15.a.7.8) 11th Battery did not fire.	
	16.11.15		Enemy Artillery again active shelling m.p. of the Canal mentioned on supply the 14th. In addition, canal bank and area in the afternoon Enemy violently trolled and also fired especially CANAL BANK area. 10th Battery again turned retaliating at request of trenches on our left. "G" & 10th Battery. 12 pounds, 11th Battery killed 6 round on train alive 14th & M.G.S. col. — Fired 34 rounds on YPRES — THEROUT Railway at (C.2.b.4.7)	
	17.11.15		working (located by P.O.P. of crane) on battery still active — Balloon up. Day very clear — always but made aerial activity.	
	18.11.15		A clear morning rain later — considerable artillery and aerial activity 10-10 AM 11th Battery did some registration with aeroplane observation. 2.30 PM Enemy shelled vicinity of 11th Battery with 20 rounds H.E. also of PELISSIER FARM and BOMBERS School (B.26.d.6.5 to B.21.c.3.10) with 25 H.E. Shell. 4.0 PM 11th Battery fired in accordance with Official Scheme. 12 Pound each on C.7.a.2.2 and FERNEL.14 (C.7.a.3.1). Fire reported to be effective but light bad to observation Enemy made aerial raid in early morning on POPERINGHE, ABEELE and neighbourhood	HKS

WAR DIARY or INTELLIGENCE SUMMARY

Army Form C. 2118
Page 4

Place	Date	Hour	Summary of Events and Information	Remarks and references to Appendices
ELVERDINGHE	19.11.15		A quieter day mainly in the afternoon. At 8.15 a.m. Enemy active with H.E. area from B.21.C.4.9 to B.20.6.5.7 - 18 shells being fired. BRIELEN Village shelled occasionally. CANAL BANK shelled all day with 77 mm Shrapnel.	
	20.11.15		Enemy Shelled all their usual targets including CANAL BANK, ELVERDINGHE and BRIELEN. 11th Bty vigorous bombardment with 40lb Shell Artillery very active.	
		12.20 and 3.20 P.M.	18th Battery shelled HIGH COMMAND REDOUBT in retaliation for 146th Inf Brigade.	
	21.11.15		Artillery again active. Enemy Shelling usual target.	
			10th Bty Pounded points with 40lb Shell firing 21 Rounds.	
	22.11.15	12.45 & 1.30 P.M.	10th Battery fired 14 Rounds retaliation & HIGH COMMAND REDOUBT and Enemy Leaders in front of D.22 for 146th Infy Brigade.	
	23.11.15		Thick mist all day - Both Batteries worked hard all over Dugouts and repair of Gun positions rendered necessary by recent heavy rains. ELVERDINGHE and BOESINGHE Another misty day. Enemy shelled ELVERDINGHE. Gun position of both Batteries	
	24.11.15		RA 2nd ARMY inspected to-day. Enemy fired over 300 shells. The major General — extreme artillery headquarters action in this area. ELVERDINGHE, PELISSIER FARM (the Brigade) a clean day. Enemy shelling ELVERDINGHE and the 4.7 and trench gun positions in our sector within the gravecourse of Headquarters similar activity on H.Q. of Infantry Battalion - old Halges [?] HALF FARM (Battalion Sector) and the 4.7 and trench gun positions in our sector repeated to 146th Infy Brigade. ESSEN FARM (146 A.S.C.) and 6 CHEMINS ESTAMINET (146.A.S.C.) 10th Battery fired 8 Rounds to 146 & Infy Brigade.	
	25.11.15	2.30 P.M.	Both Batteries did some registration. Hostile Balloons up. A few other kept a quieter day - Enemy Shelled BOESINGHE, BRIELEN and a few other french trenches in second area with C.F.A. No 506 on front in enemy shells 148th Inf 10th Battery fired 6 Rounds (in second area with C.F.A. No 506) on front in enemy shells 148 Inf Reported by Boad [?] Instructor upon hostility and recent enemy fire in this by C.R.A's orders - the R[?] Brigade Halges. And at 10.35 in retaliation for HIGH COMMAND REDOUBT and the hostile Trenches - the 11th Battery	
		10.35	fired 50 Rounds & HIGH COMMAND REDOUBT and the hostile Zone fired 18 Rounds to points in their Zone. On heavy artillery fired upon the enemy artillery indicated as above, but apparently did not cease firing	HMS

1577 Wt.W10791/1773 500,000 1/15   D. D. & L.   A.D.S.S./Forms/C. 2118.

WAR DIARY
or
INTELLIGENCE SUMMARY.

(Erase heading not required.)

Army Form C. 2118.

5.

Place	Date	Hour	Summary of Events and Information	Remarks and references to Appendices
ELVERDINGHE	26/11/15		A fairly quiet day – ELVERDINGHE CHATEAU Ground Shelled with 10 rounds from H.V. Gun fitted to battery front. The Divisional Commander inspected the Gun Positions.	
"	27/11/15		An exceedingly quiet day – hard frost. 11th Battery fired 8 rounds at parents on enemy trenches when work was suspected.	
"	28th/11		During the morning it was too misty to observe.	
		3.5 pm	In the afternoon 10th R.F.A. reported VON SPEE with aeroplane observation. There was a certain amount of hostile shelling during the day.	
"	29/11	12.20 pm	10th R.F.A. fired 14 rounds on a Trench mortar at C14.b.9.4 at rounds at Infantry. The mortar was silenced. 11th R.F.A. fired 4 rounds at CECAM FARM (C80.E.3) when no hostile shelling during the day.	
"	30/11	8.55 am	10th R.F.A. fired 6 rounds at report of hit infront of D21 & D22.	
		1.0 m	" " Registered C14.a.33 C15.a.11 C14.b.92.1	
		2.30	Retaliated at 1.15 pm infront of E27 fired 10 rounds.	
		11.0 am	11th R.F.A. Registered C7.d.8.5 & 8.6.	

H.K. Stephenson

Fis. w. Chi. Psx. R.F.A.

Dec 1915

vol VI

49

WAR DIARY
or
INTELLIGENCE SUMMARY.

Army Form C. 2118.

CONFIDENTIAL

WAR DIARY

OF

4TH WEST RIDING (HOWITZER) BDE, R.F.A

From 1-12-15. To 31-12-15.

(VOLUME VI)

Army Form C. 2118.

WAR DIARY
or
INTELLIGENCE SUMMARY.
(Erase heading not required.)

Page 1

Instructions regarding War Diaries and Intelligence Summaries are contained in F. S. Regs., Part II. and the Staff Manual respectively. Title pages will be prepared in manuscript.

Place	Date	Hour	Summary of Events and Information	Remarks and references to Appendices
ELVERDINGHE	1.12.15		A day of great artillery activity – The Enemy shelled all their favourite targets, putting some 200 shell (H.E) in the area between ELVERDINGHE and BRIELEN (incl.).	MAP BELGIUM B SERIES SHEET 28 N.W.
		2.0 p.m.	The 10th & 11th R Batteries each fired 40 Rounds on HIGH COMMAND REDOUBT in accordance with instructions for a combined Bombardment by Heavy Batteries – The F.O.O.'s reported effect very good.	
	2.12.15		10th Battery fired intermittently on points Bombarded previous day. Hostile shelling – very little effect under operators orders	
		12.0 noon	11th Battery fired 25 rounds on ZOUAVE HOUSE (C.7.b.2½.8½) – Fire reported effective. 11th Battery also registered with aeroplane observation C.14.a.8.5 (Cross Roads) and C.2.c.8.5 (Cross Roads) – Both satisfactory	
	3.12.15		A quiet day – little hostile shelling – neither Battery fired	
	4.12.15 11/30 a.m.		Enemy shelled in front of 10th Battery position (8 Rounds 4.2 H.E) then turned on to 11th Battery position (10 rounds)	
		2.45 p.m.	Enemy fired 24 H.E. shell from High Velocity guns in neighbourhood of Brewery (B.15.d.2.2)	
		3.20 p.m.	10th Battery fired 10 rounds on HIGH COMMAND REDOUBT and 2 Rounds on Enemy trenches in front of D.20 at request of 146th Infty. Brigade – Result reported effective.	
Sat	5.12.15 12.10 a.m.		Enemy put 19 shell into ELVERDINGHE – some blind, remainder very weak burst	
		4.45 p.m. onwards	ELVERDINGHE – BRIELEN road persistently shelled. 10th Battery fired occasional rounds (8) on Enemy trenches fronting D.21 during night 11th Battery registered trenches C.14. a.2.6, a.2.4, a.2.6, and a.3.4½	24/5/22
	6.12.15		A fairly quiet day – 1.20 p.m. 10th Battery at request of 146th Infty. Brigade fired 6 rounds at KRUPP FARM (recent rebuilding). Same Battery also fired during night 5/6/15 occasional Rounds on Enemy trenches opposite D.20	

HHS

1577 Wt.W10791/1773 500,000 1/15 D.D. & L. A.D.S.S./Forms/C. 2118.

WAR DIARY or INTELLIGENCE SUMMARY

Army Form C. 2118
Page 2

Place	Date	Hour	Summary of Events and Information	Remarks and references to Appendices
ELVERDINGHE	7.12.15		Hostile Artillery active all day. Battery positions round ELVERDINGHE received special attention - also a good deal of shelling in the neighbourhood of the 10th By Battery Gun position and billets. - Enemy Aircraft active.	
		10.0 A.M. 5.0 P.M.	10th Battery fired 8 occasional rounds on HIGH COMMAND REDOUBT and with aeroplane observation registered satisfactorily C.14.a.7½.0 and C.14.a.9½.1 firing 19 rounds.	
	8.12.15		Clear day with great artillery activity on both sides. Both Batteries in conjunction with Heavy Batteries took part in bombardment of Enemy Trenches to the left of HIGH COMMAND REDOUBT firing 90 rounds in all. Results subsequently reported very satisfactory.	
		11.10 A.M.	10th Battery fired 32 rounds on 2nd line trench E.14.a.6.8 and C.7.d.9.½ also 12 rounds on C.7.d.9.1 at request of 145th Infty. Brigade 11th Battery fired 59 rounds at request of same Brigade on 2nd line Trenches C.8.c.1.2 to C.8.c.1.4. - This retaliation reported effective.	
		1.15 P.M.	10th Battery fired 6 rounds. By O.C. Brigade order (received from A.R.A.) on C.8.b.4.2 C.9.a.2.5 and C.9.c.d.15.7 which provoked immediate enemy retaliation. Considerable aeroplane activity during day - Enemy shelled Elverdinghe all day in this area putting 134 H.E. Shells on 2nd W.R. Battery position near Brewery.	
	9.12.15		Both Batteries fired occasional rounds during the night on HIGH COMMAND REDOUBT and other specified points as ordered by C.R.A.	
		5.0 A.M. 5.20.5	Enemy opened heavy bombardment on trenches held by 145th Infty Brigade Received Retaliation Call 10th Battery fired 56 rounds on Second Line trenches C.14.a. C.9.d.1.2 to C.9.c.14.	
		6.0 A.M.	11th Battery fired 52 rounds on 2nd Line Trenches C.8.c.1.2 to C.8.c.14. After considerable retaliation by our Heavy Batteries Enemy fire ceased Remainder of day quiet.	

HRS

WAR DIARY or INTELLIGENCE SUMMARY

Army Form C. 2118

Page 3

Place	Date	Hour	Summary of Events and Information	Remarks and references to Appendices
ELVERDINGHE	10.12.15		Both Batteries fired occasional rounds during night as before - Enemy shells in front of 10th Battery during day - a fairly quiet day	
	11.12.15	3.05 a.m	Enemy shelled whole area between BRIELEN and ELVERDINGHE for about 15 minutes each hour. At about 7.10 a.m. this billet was hit by 4.2" Howr. H.E. shell and another fell in garden 25 yds. S. Others fell over - no casualties material damage slight. The wood S. of ELVERDINGHE was shelled intermittently - 45 shells both H.E. and S. being fired.	
	12.12.15	11.30 am 3.0 pm	10th Battery fired occasional rounds during night 10/11th as before. A good deal of artillery activity - Enemy put 30 rounds chiefly H.E. in front of ELVERDINGHE Brewery between 10.0 a.m. and 1.0 p.m. PELISSIER and HALE Farms (B.20.d.8.10 and B.20.d.7.9) were also shelled and 4 shells fell just in front of this Billet (B.20.8.8.9)	
		3.0 to 4.30 pm	Hostile balloon up. Hostile shelling - Some aeroplane activity - Rather less hostile shelling -	
	13.12.15	11.40 am 12.57 pm 2.20 pm 4.10 pm	10th Battery fired 9 rounds on Enemy trenches C.14.b.9.3 to C.14.b.3.3 to silence trench mortar - 146th Infy Brigade reported trench mortar silenced 10th Battery fired 4 rounds on C.15.a.7.8 at request of 146th Infy Brigade By order of C.R.A. 10th Battery opened fire on Enemy trench C.9.a.2.8 After 1st round Enemy artillery opened on Battery - no casualties	
	14.12.15	4.30 pm	A quiet morning but considerable aerial activity. In the afternoon some hostile shelling on the ELVERDINGHE area (in the neighbourhood of the BREWERY and in the direction of 6" and 4.7 Gun positions and near our Hd.Qr Billet (B.14.d.10.3) 20 small pieces of H.E. shell and 2 shrapnel between B.22.d.10.4 and B.28.b.10.3 (B.20 central)	
	15.12.15		A good deal of hostile shelling behind our trenches on Battery positions and in our area - ELVERDINGHE, BRIELEN to Yser. Battery fired.	
	16.12.15		Great artillery activity. Between noon and 4.0 p.m. noon and between 12.20 and 12.30 Enemy Shelled ELVERDINGHE BREWERY (B.15.c.6.5) PELISSIER FARM (B.21.c.2.10) HALE FARM (B.22.d.7.8) and the fields round about as well as the corner of ELVERDINGHE near	

HKS

WAR DIARY or INTELLIGENCE SUMMARY

Army Form C. 2118
Page 4

Place	Date	Hour	Summary of Events and Information	Remarks and references to Appendices
ELVERDINGHE	16.12.15	cont.	near the Water Tower with some 400 shells of various kinds — the vicinity of BRIELEN experienced a similar bombardment.	
		2.5 P.M.	10th OB battery fired 6 rounds at the request of the 146th Infy Brigade on C.15.a.6.8 in retaliation for enemy shelling of LA BELLE ALLIANCE FARM	
		3.20 P.M.	The enemy fire then increased and firing ceased at 3.20 P.M. retaliation on C.14.b.6.4 was requested and 6 rounds fired — at 4.0 P.M. 2nd Sea Brigade	
		4.0 P.M.	requested retaliation on C.15.A.0.3 — 4 rounds fired — No further retaliation needed.	
	17.12.15		A good deal of hostile shelling on trenches & rear behind.	
		11.45 A.M.	10 shell 5.9 H.E. fell in course of ELVERDINGHE (about B.12.d.9.9.)	
		8.50 A.M.	10th Battery fired 8 rounds on HIGH COMMAND REDOUBT (C.14.L.9.3) at request of 146th Infy Brigade — Infantry reports retaliation effective.	
		10.30 A.M.	10th Battery fired 17 rounds on Support Trench (C.14.a.4.6¾) at request of 148th Infy Brigade — Infantry quite satisfied.	
		10.20	10th Battery fired 7.14 rounds Lyd.& (140lb) shell and 56 Many (30lb) on second line of HIGH COMMAND REDOUBT opposite D21 and D22 — at 11.45 A.M.	
		11.25 A.M.	Bde of HIGH COMMAND REDOUBT opposite D21 and D22 — at 11.45 A.M. on Infantry reported cessation of hostile fire	
		11.10 A.M.	11th Battery by order of O.C. Brigade (on orders received from C.R.A.) fired 25 rounds on 2nd line Trenches from C.14.a.6.8 to C.14.a.9.7 and 24 rounds on trenches from C.14.a.3.5 to C.14.a.2.6 by order of O.C. Brigade on orders from C.R.A.	
	18.12.15		A misty day — slow hostile shelling — neither heavy fired.	
	19.12.15	3.45 a.m. 5.30	Infantry reported gas attack which was accompanied by heavy bombardment of our trenches — 10th Battery ordered to open fire on HIGH COMMAND REDOUBT and Reserve trenches opposite to 148th Infy Brigade which had requested retaliation, 10th Battery in vicinity fired 119 rounds. 11th Battery tapped telephone message from Infantry reporting	HKS

WAR DIARY
or
INTELLIGENCE SUMMARY
(Erase heading not required.)

Army Form C. 2118

Page 5

Place	Date	Hour	Summary of Events and Information	Remarks and references to Appendices
ELVERDINGHE	19/12/15	5.50 A.M.	Gas and immediately opened fire on FERME 14 (C.7.c.4.6) and T (C.7.c.7.9)	
		5.55	On instructions from C.R.A. O.C. 11th Brigade ordered 11th Battery to turn fire on to Enemy front parapet at KIEL COTTAGE (C.7.d.5.6) and at C.7.c.8.5	
		6.30	On instructions from C.R.A. O.C. 11th Brigade ordered 11th Battery to turn fire on to trenches C.14.a.3.5 and C.14.a.2.8 (Section fire 2 minutes)	
		7.0	O.C. 11th Brigade ordered 10th Battery to turn fire on front parapet at KIEL COTTAGE from C.7.d.5.6 to C.7.d.8.5 (Section fire 3 minutes)	
			About this time Enemy began to bombard all Roads and Battery positions in rear of our trenches — 10 H.E. & 2 Contrelos (?) (7 min) Shells fell on and round ELVERDINGHE (from B.14.d. b.4.t., B.14.c.7.1	
		P.M. 2.15	10th Battery at request of 148th Infantry Brigade retaliated with 15 rounds on Enemy second line trenches near ESSEN FARM (C.14.a.6.2)	
		3.25	O.C. Brigade in instructions from C.R.A. ordered 10th Battery to retaliate on HIGH COMMAND REDOUBT — 21 rounds fired — infantry satisfied	
		3.0	11th Battery at request of 148th Infantry Bgde. fired 6 rounds on Enemy 2nd line trench (Apont P. 28)	
		3.35	11th Battery received further reports from 148th Infy. Bgde. and retaliated	
		9.30	11th Battery by request of same Infy. Bgde. fired 8 rounds on Communication trench (C.14.c.7.3)	
		11.25	11th Battery on further report of gas (which turned out to be unfounded) fired 27 rounds on Enemy front parapet (C.7.d.8.5)	
		11.40	On similar report O.C. Brigade ordered 10th Battery to fire on HIGH COMMAND REDOUBT (C.14.B.9.3) and Second line trenches — 24 rounds fired.	
			During the whole day & through the night no much obs between Batteries further than the 10th Battery fired 2.14 rounds and during the night 5.30 a.m. to midnight the 10th Battery fired 2.14 rounds.	

HKL

Army Form C. 2118

Page 6

WAR DIARY
or
INTELLIGENCE SUMMARY
(Erase heading not required.)

Place	Date	Hour	Summary of Events and Information	Remarks and references to Appendices
ELVERDINGHE	19.12.15		The 11th Battery 194 rounds. The 11th Battery had 3 casualties - 1 man gassed, 4 men wounded by shell fire. They had also 1 gun put out of action by a direct hit which went through the case and brought down barrage to gun (reported alight). The gas attack in the morning was prepared only on retaliation but the enemy knew their trenches but were unable to advance or fire. The hostile artillery fire was active all day and night all road being under continual shell fire. Day was very clear.	
	20.12.15		we the enemy had 3 (Atwoolen, Baloons &c) which enabled them to keep our roads under observation. Hostile aeroplane active all day. During the day the wind changed from W.E. to N.N.E. In the afternoon & evening the wind enabled to all parts statistic and the C.R.A. enough of stench the temp statistic to all parts & the C.R.A. from the Divisional commander and the C.R.A. thick mist which lasted till dark resulted in a comparatively quiet	
		3.15 P.M.	day. As required of 145th Infantry Brigade 11th Battery fired 12 rounds (C.8.c.5.E.) on enemy trench at C.14.a.6.8, 9,7	
		3.30	11th Battery an similar target fired 12 rounds on MACKENSEN FARM (C.8.c.5.E.)	
		3.30	10th Battery on Sniper of 146th Infantry Bde. fired 12 rounds on second line trenches behind Western portion of HIGH COMMAND REDOUBT (C.14.b.9.3)	
		3.50	11th Battery ordered by O.C. Bgde. on instructions from C.R.A. to join on C.14.a.6.8.-9.-7 and EOLYAN FARM (C.8.C.2.5) - 10 rounds fired on each target.	
	21.12.15		During the night the enemy indulged in promiscuous shelling between BRIELEN and ELVERDINGHE inclusive especially on the roads. Gun shell being particularly used. – a hot day not much artillery activity.	
		4.15 A.M.	10th Battery fired 19 rounds on 2nd line trenches W. of H.C. REDOUBT (C.14.8.9.3) at request of 146th Infantry Brigade	

JMS

Army Form C. 2118

Page 7

WAR DIARY
or
INTELLIGENCE SUMMARY
(Erase heading not required.)

Instructions regarding War Diaries and Intelligence Summaries are contained in F.S. Regs., Part II and the Staff Manual respectively. Title Pages will be prepared in manuscript.

Place	Date	Hour	Summary of Events and Information	Remarks and references to Appendices
ELVERDINGHE	22.12.15		A dull day. Rainy. not much artillery activity.	
		11.55	10th Battery fired 4 rounds on communication trench opposite E.29 at the request of 148th Infy Brigade who observed movement in enemy trenches between points c.9.d.2.5 to c.7.d.9.1	
		12.5	11th Battery fired 6 rounds on enemy trench between points c.9.d.2.5 to c.7.d.9.1	
			at request of 143rd Infty Bgde. in same sector.	
		12.20	Enemy fired 100 H.E. Shells into areas B.15.a, B.15.c, B.20.b and B.21.a	
	23.12.15		Hostile Artillery active behind our trenches. During the day the following places amongst others were shelled. BRIELEN—ELVERDINGHE ROAD, FANTASIA FARM (with 13 Salvoes) (B.21.d.7.9), ELVERDINGHE BREWERY (B.15.c.5.5), and between 2.30 + 4.0 P.M. in reply to the fire of our Heavies the enemy artillery recopies and searched the countryside from BRIELEN to ELVERDINGHE enclosure found a large number of shells. 10th Battery fired 48 rounds on second line trench at c.14.a.2.5.6.2 and R.O.W. FARM (c.14.a.8.6) at request of 148th Infty Brigade. "Retaliation effective"	
		1.15 P.M.		
	24.12.15		A quiet day. Enemy put 9 rounds between 1.0 and 2.30 P.M. June and Concarneau H.E. between B.15.c.1.7 (just behind the B.E.at) and ELVERDINGHE WHITETOWER (B.14.d.7.4) and ELVERDINGHE CHATEAU GROUNDS (B.14.8.5)	
		2.45 P.M and 6.5 P.M.	H.E. on edge of ELVERDINGHE CHATEAU GROUNDS (B.14.8.5)	
			neither Battery fired.	
	25.12.15		Xmas Day — a certain amount of violated shelling occasionally done to some of our Field Batteries firing on parties of enemy at 5.30 a.m. In retaliation enemy fired 92 H.E. Shell June and Concarneau but chiefly the latter in ELVERDINGHE BREWERY (B.15.a.7.5)	
	26.12.15		A clear day but high wind — Hostile Airplane active in morning. Our trenches. Enemy put 35 H.E. Percuss Shells on FANTASIA FARM (B.21.d.8.7) and 30 obs in front of ELVERDINGHE BREWERY (B.15.c.5.5)	
			neither Battery fired.	
				HKS

WAR DIARY
or
INTELLIGENCE SUMMARY
(Erase heading not required.)

Army Form C. 2118

Page 5

Place	Date	Hour	Summary of Events and Information	Remarks and references to Appendices
ELVERDINGHE	27.12.15	6.30 A.M.	2 Salvoes 7.7cm H.E. burst short of Hetty Brigade Hdqrs. Billet (B.14.d.9.1) PELISSIER FARM (B.21.c.2.10), ELVERDINGHE BREWERY (B.15.c.6.3), ELVERDINGHE – BRIELEN ROAD Shelled during day	
		4.57 P.M.	10th Battery fired 12 rounds retaliation on HIGH COMMAND REDOUBT (C.14.b.9.3) at request of 146th Infty. Brigade	
		2.30 P.M.	Above retaliation repeated with 8 rounds – Infantry satisfied. 110th Battery did not fire.	
	28.12.15		A fine clear day with considerable aerial and artillery activity – 80 H.E. shells burst near ELVERDINGHE BREWERY (B.15.c.7.6) between 11.30 and 1.60 a.m. Between 3.10 and 5.0, 330 H.E. shells (new and obvious burst) burst near FANTASIA and PIONEER FARMS (B.21.d) – At 5.57 P.M. a further 50 shell H.E. and S. burst in front of the BREWERY.	
		12.27 P.M.	10th Battery ordered on instructions from C.R.A. to retaliate on Enemy front line trench from C.14.b.9.3 to C.14.b.2.5 – 30 rounds fired	
	29.12.15		Hostile Artillery active on ELVERDINGHE, BRIELEN and Battery positions near village	
		1.0 to 2.30 P.M.	H.E. Shell burst on ELVERDINGHE Chateau Grounds (B.16.c.7.5) – 5 Heavy (12"?) – 25 H.E. 5".9 fell in a line from the ELVERDINGHE – HOSPITAL FARM ROAD (B.14 Central) – to just beyond the S.E. corner of this billet (B.14.d.9.1) The nearest shell falling 6 yards from the house. 4 June H.E. shell burst between this billet and fire.	
			3rd W.R.Bde. R.F.A. Hd.Qrs. (B.15-c.16)	
			10th Battery fired in retaliation at 6.45 h.m. the previous night (28th) this fire 5 rounds on second line trenches opposite E.24, 25, + 26 on receipt of "YA'S S.O.S." Call from 146th Infty. Brigade – This turned out to be a false alarm. On June Call 11th Battery fired 4 rounds in trench C.14.a.2.6	

HMS

WAR DIARY or INTELLIGENCE SUMMARY

Army Form C. 2118

Page 9

Place	Date	Hour	Summary of Events and Information	Remarks and references to Appendices
ELVERDINGHE	30.12.15	A.M. 11.0	A quieter day - 2 High velocity guns firing on POPERINGHE at intervals during day.	
	31.12.15	2.0 P.M.	14th DIVISION took over command of line. In accordance with orders one section each of 10th and 11th Batteries withdrawn to Woesten Lines being replaced by 2 sections of the 49th Bde. R.F.A. 14th Div. In accordance with orders handed over Billet, Telephone lines to Col. Dowell R.A. Comdg. 49th Brigade R.F.A. and withdrew to 49th Div. C.R.A.'s Hdqrs. preparatory to movement of Brigade to Rest area when 14th Div Batteries completed registration.	

HWStephenson
LIEUT. COL. R.F.A.
COMDG. 4TH W. R. (HOWZR.) BDE. R.F.A.

121/6344

49th Division

4th W.R. Bde R.F.A.

Vol I

14-5-15 31-7-15

Army Form C. 2118.

WAR DIARY
or
INTELLIGENCE SUMMARY.
(Erase heading not required.)

CONFIDENTIAL

WAR DIARY

OF

4TH WEST RIDING (HOWITZER) BDE, R.F.A.

from 14-5-15 to 31-7-15.

(Volume I)

Page 1

Army Form C. 2118.

Instructions regarding War Diaries and Intelligence Summaries are contained in F.S. Regs., Part II. and the Staff Manual respectively. Title pages will be prepared in manuscript.

WAR DIARY
4th W. Riding or (How) Bde R.F.A
INTELLIGENCE SUMMARY. 10th W. Batt[?] 11th [?] Amm. Column
4TH WEST RIDING (HOWITZER) BDE, R.F.A.

Place	Date	Hour	Summary of Events and Information	Remarks and references to Appendices
DONCASTER	14.5.15 / 15.5.15	11pm to 4am	The unit consisting of sixteen Officers 392 other ranks under the command of Lieut Col H.K. Stephenson, R.P.A.(T) left Doncaster in three trains for SOUTHAMPTON, embarked on a hired transport S.S. ANGLO-CANADIAN at 8pm & reached HAVRE the early morning of the 16.5.15. Disembarked & spent the day in the docks.	
	15.5.15	—	One slight casualties occurred during the disembarkation of the guns. the horses attached to the trail of a gun broke, when the gun was about 12ft from the ground & the trail swung on & struck Gnr Barker. & Spr Ledger of the A.C. These men were left at HAVRE.	
SVENANT	17.5.15		The unit entrained in 3 trains at 8pm at point no. 3. each train took 24 hours to reach BOURGETTE when each battery marched into billets 1 mile W of SVENANT.	
—	18.5.15		The Unit remained at SVENANT until the morning of the 25.5.15 when they were attached to R.A. 1st DIVISION	
—	25.5.15	8am	The unit marched via ROBECQ — ST VENANT — MT BERENCHON — LE CORNET MALO to LA TOMBE WILLOT where the Bde billeted for the night.	
RICHBOURG ST VAAST	26.5.15 / 27.5.15		The gunners of the 10th & 11th Batteries Batteries marched to RICHBOURG — ST VAAST. & prepared their gun positions. The A.C. & bage. lines remained at LA-TOMBE-WILLOT. HdQtrs remained in RICHBOURG village	
	29.5.15		Batteries commenced registering on zones allied. Observation Station on the RUE du BOIS. E of the MILL.	
	9.5.15	5am	The Unit took part in the heavy bombardment carried out this day by the 1st Division. The unit fired about 1200 rounds of LYDDITE between the hours of 5am & 8pm.	
	10.5.15		The Artillery of the 1st Div. & their attached were banked in a general order issued by Gen Hankin Cmdt 1st Div. for the unit carried out by them on the 9th inst.	
	11.5.15	—	nil	
	12.5.15		A steady bombardment at the rate of 3 rounds per battery per hour was issued against the enemies rear trenches between WINDY CORNER & the road between [illegible] & the 11th Battery, killing No 1102 Br Fairburn	
	13.5.15	6pm	A shell burst on the rear between 4774 Br Brayshaw (slightly) 10th L.R. Batt., & wounding 10th L.R. Batty.	
	18.5.15		Intermittent fire during day at enemys front & rear trenches. & during the night of 13th Ins[?]	

H.K.S. Lt Col

Army Form C. 2118.

WAR DIARY
4th W.R. or (How) Bde R.F.A.
INTELLIGENCE SUMMARY.
(Erase heading not required.)

10th W.R. Regt
11th Do
Amm. Column

Place	Date	Hour	Summary of Events and Information	Remarks and references to Appendices
RICHBOURG S' VAAST	14.5.15	—	Same as on 13.5.15 but alloc of 50 rds a gun per day reduced to 25 rds.	
	15.5.15	—	B. alloc & Amm. revised to 50 rds.	
	"	11.30pm	Two stopped preliminary assault. Batteries ready all through the night. Fire 2/3rd at various hours on objectives set out in a programme.	
	16.5.15	12 midday	Expenditure of Ammn up to 12 midday 516 Rds. Casualties: No 803 Gr. STOCKDALE 11th Batt wounded.	
	"	10 pm	Night lines arranged.	to 11th Batt. 3 Rds per battery per hour during the night 16.17
	17.5.15	9 am	Intermittent firing on certain objectives.	detailed to observe fire.
	18.5.15		Intermittent firing From du Bois + Tome de TOLOTTE	
	19.5.15		Indian troops took over portion E.R. Border Track + we hence forth called the Right group from Richbourg P.18 + P.16 + supp Hop. A 21 N20	
	20.5.15		Intermittent firing at targets on the front front.	
	21.5.15		Do	
	22.5.15	7.10 am	Received task of fire of Town a height. My 10 rounds after an infantry attack on Fm du Bois.	
		11 am	Orders to join 49th Division	Baggage & stores slow coming up from fire. Baggage waggons in a field
FLEURBAIX	22.5.15	3.30	Left Richbourg + marched via FOSSE — LA GORGUE — BAC B HAVRE — began new march from Sailly area. Next day. On arrival at Mt Olivin billets arranged.	
			E15 R BAC B HAVRE H 15 & 9.7 became the Bac Position. Am Column Coy.	
		2 pm	Batteries moved up S of FLEUR BAIX + commenced digging in.	
do	23.5.15	—	Commenced Registering	
	24.5.15	8 pm	Bombardment by Artillery og supp of enemy's trenches + various objective points. The night 24/25. In particular a house which has been barricaded in the enemy's held 7 Sillini &	
	25.5.15		Special target to Mt Sailly a house which has been barricaded, a hard target 3 hits time allowed, windows held, motor, a hard target. 11 Sailli also ranged on this house in the minute	
	26.5.15		Same as on 25th.	

HHA/L Lt.

WAR DIARY or INTELLIGENCE SUMMARY

Army Form C. 2118. Page 3.

Place	Date	Hour	Summary of Events and Information	Remarks and references to Appendices
FLEURBAIX	26.5.	8pm	Lt. F. C. E. Peterson arrived from Meerut Divn. on attachment as adjutant.	
"	26.5-27.5	10.6pm	10th By moved into position about 3/4 mile away.	
"	27.5.	1.15pm	11th By turned on to new trench opposite no 6 Trench & fired 24 rounds.	
"	28.5.		During the morning the advanced section of the 11th By registered a few prominent points on their line.	
"	"	3.0pm	13th By fired a few rounds on hostile trench at the spot after infantry	
"	29.5.	5.45pm	10th By fired two rounds at enemy's trench near point 863 on orders received from C.R.A.	
"	"	9.0pm	Remaining 5 of the 11th By moved up to advanced position.	
"	30.5.15	12.30am	10th By fired 8 rounds searching road behind german lines from pt. 863 to ROUGE BANCS.	
"	"		During the day 10th By continued to register. 11th By completed communications.	
"	"		" " "	
"	31.5.		Both batteries continued registration.	
"	1/6/15		" " "	
"	2/6/15	11.0 am	10th By fires on cupola at 863. Considerable trouble experienced with telephone line to OP.	

HWSLee

WAR DIARY or INTELLIGENCE SUMMARY

Army Form C. 2118.

Page 4

Place	Date	Hour	Summary of Events and Information	Remarks and references to Appendices
FLEURBAIX	3/6/15		11h 35 registered cupola at 983.	
"	4/6/		Both batteries continued registration & also worked on fire pits.	
"	5/6/		No firing	
"	6/6/		" "	
"	7/6/	2.30pm	O.C. R.H.a inspected wagon line of batteries & gun teams	
"	8/6/		No firing	
"	9/6/		10h 15 no firing.	
"	"		Fired 3 rounds at cupola at 883 & 3 rounds at 880.	
"	10/6/	10.20a	11h 00 Completed registration	
"	"	9.30a	10h 15 moved about 3 miles to a new position at M6a covering under command of C.R.a. 8th Division Citeres no adjusting on tactical entrances	
"	11/6/		No firing FERME DELANGRE.	
"	12/6/		" " "	
"	13/6/		" " "	
"	14/6/		" " "	
"	15/6/		" " "	
"	16/6/		" " "	
"	17/6/	3.0pm	11h Reg registering	
"	18/6/		No firing	
"	19/6/		" "	
"	20/6/		" "	
"	21/6/		"	

Army Form C. 2118.

Page 5.

WAR DIARY
or
INTELLIGENCE SUMMARY.
(Erase heading not required.)

Instructions regarding War Diaries and Intelligence Summaries are contained in F.S. Regs., Part II. and the Staff Manual respectively. Title pages will be prepared in manuscript.

Place	Date	Hour	Summary of Events and Information	Remarks and references to Appendices
FLEURBAIX	22/6/-	10.30am.	11th Bty fired 12 rounds at hostile battery in square N23d 77 and silenced it.	
"	"	9.30pm.	10th Bty returned to its former position & came under Bde Tactical Control after 13th.	
"	23/6/-		No firing.	
"	24/6/-		" " "	
"	25/6/-		" " "	
"	26/6/-		Adjutant went on a week's leave to England.	
"	27/6/-	5.0pm.	11th Bty fired 12 rounds at hostile bty at N23d 3.3½ (36 N.W.)	
"	"	8.30pm	Bde HQ 10th & 11th Batteries left their positions 0 mins to rest area G.21.a.5.0 (HQ) — 10th (G.21.a.57) & 11th (G.21.a.37) arriving their new area G.21.a.5.0 (HQ) — Bde A.C. remained at G.10.a.2.4.	
REST AREA near BAC ST MAUR	28/6/-	10.30 pm	Rested & overhauled equipment etc.	
"	29/6/-			
"	30/6/-	7.0pm	Bde received orders to proceed with 48th Divn to join 6th Corps. Marched from billets at 7.0pm. Passed O.C. 1st W.R.Bde west of ESTAIRES. Left under his orders at 8.0pm. for CAESTRE arriving there at 11.30 pm. Billeted there for the night.	HWA Lt. Col.

Army Form C. 2118.

Page 6.

WAR DIARY
or
INTELLIGENCE SUMMARY.
(Erase heading not required.)

Place	Date	Hour	Summary of Events and Information	Remarks and references to Appendices
CAESTRE	1-7-15	8pm	March resumed at 2.0 p.m. to WATAU & HOUTKERQUE arriving between 11pm & 12 midnight. H.Q. at E.22.d.10.6; 10th at E.15.d.3.1; 11th at E.22.a.17 & Amm Col E.23.d.s.o. (Sheet 27)	
WATAU	2/7/15		Bde rested near WATAU	
"	3/7/15		" " " Adjutant returned from leave.	
"	4/7/15		" " " Bde Commander & B.C's went up in motor lorries to reconnoitre Bty positions near BRIELEN.	
"	5/7/15		Bde rested + B.C's took up digging parties.	
"	6/7/15	9.0pm	On the night of 6/7. 1 X 11"How & 1 X Ammn Col. moved up to new area at L3b (Sheet 27) while O.C. 10th Bty took up a digging party to prepare Bty position.	
"	7/7/15		During the day O.C. 10th reconnoitred a wagon line & during the evening at 9.0pm the remainder of 11"How & Ammn Col. moved up to new area	
		9.0pm	together with the 10th Bde. One sec of 11"How & Bde A.C. came up into action – 11"How at B.27.d.94 (sheet 28 N.W.) this position has previously been occupied by 96th composite Bde. (4.5's.)	
			In H.Q. moves to BRIELEN.	

MR Lt Col

WAR DIARY or INTELLIGENCE SUMMARY.

Army Form C. 2118.

Page 7

Place	Date	Hour	Summary of Events and Information	Remarks and references to Appendices
BRIELEN	8/7/15	9.0.p.m	During the day 11th Bty reported with its X in action & during the night at 9.0 p.m. remainder of 11th & 8th Bn at Cerne up. Also me & 8th P5 came up to its action at B 23 c 63 to a new position during the day.	
"	9/7/15		During the day both batteries continued registering. Remainder of	
"	10/7/15	9.30 p	10th Bty Cerne up into action at 9.30 p.m.	
"	15/7/15		During the day both batteries continued registering. The 10th Bty fired 15 hostile Trench near WIELTJE COTT & fired 12 rounds in answer to hostile 5.9" shelling of our Trenches.	
"		7.40 p.m	At 7.40 p.m 11th Bty F.O.O. observed enemy running down comm. Trench at 'T' & 1st Bns fire on them, considerable after 115 rounds fire information was received that enemy has made trench at 'T' & 11th Bty fire 30 seconds at 6.15 pm an aeroplane sincer. At 6.50 information was	
"		8.30 p	was turned on to this shell fire X fire range was increased on information received that her per after trench was recaptured.	

HWA 2/Lt. Col

Army Form C. 2118.

WAR DIARY
or
INTELLIGENCE SUMMARY.
(Erase heading not required.)

Page 6

Place	Date	Hour	Summary of Events and Information	Remarks and references to Appendices
BRIELEN	11/7/15	9pm	11th RFA continues firing at same rate except for 3 salvos at 9.15pm.	
		10.30	At 10.45pm rate of fire was reduced to see fire 1 run. At 10.30 emptied guns 9 shots by.	
"	11/7/15	-	Both batteries continues registering. After rapid fire positions were also worked in.	
"	"	9pm	In the evening 10th RFA fired two salvos at 'T'.	
"	12/7/15	-	Both batteries continued registering.	
"	"	6.0pm	10th RFA fired 4 bog rounds at 'T' in reply to german shelling of our trenches. At the same time 11th RFA also fires observed enemy at 'T' & fired a few rounds at KIEL COTT.	
"	"	9pm	11th RFA fired 6 fly cuts near CHATEAU DES TROIS TOURS.	
"	13/7/15	6.0am	11th RFA fired 4 rounds at 'T' — retaliation. During the day both batteries registered.	
"	"	7.30pm	F.O.O. 11th RFA reports hostile fire rather heavy in the neighbourhood of FME 14 'T' & about 200 yds to the right of 'T'.	HMAH LR

1577 Wt. W10791/1773 500,000 1/15 D. D. & L. A.D.S.S./Forms/C. 2118.

Army Form C. 2118.

Page 9

WAR DIARY
or
INTELLIGENCE SUMMARY.
(Erase heading not required.)

Place	Date	Hour	Summary of Events and Information	Remarks and references to Appendices
BRIELEN	13/7/17	7.30h	B.C. was preparing to open fire in retaliation on KIEL COTT when orders were received from CRA to fire a German Trench mortar FME 14 + a FME 14 salt.	
"	"	7.45h	F.O.O. 9/76th Bty reported hostile activity in own vicinity & O.C. wrote likewise goes to so that when orders were received both batteries open fire without delay.	
"	"	7.15p	Orders reached the batteries at 7.50 & fire was open at the rate of X rds 30". Fire was directed on 'FME 14'-'T' & German front line Trench in that neighbourhood, also in the common French running behind + just above the eye of FME 14. Both F.O.O's were so just able to observe & cover their fire through little correction was found necessary but after a short time the view became obscured by smoke & smother of time barriers & in	
"	"	8.0h	F.O.O. 15th reported to cnts observe no movement in that observation owing to dusk.	HHA/4. Col

1577 Wt. W10791/1773 500,000 1/15 D. D. & L. A.D.S.S./Forms/C. 2118.

Army Form C. 2118.

Page 10

WAR DIARY
or
INTELLIGENCE SUMMARY.
(Erase heading not required.)

Place	Date	Hour	Summary of Events and Information	Remarks and references to Appendices
BRIELEN	13/7/-	8·0h to 6.28p	F.O.O. reports that white lights & later red lights were sent up from German lines. F.O.O. 11th RFA reports that several of the infantry retired past his O.P. in different stages of asphyxiation	
"	"	8.38p	O.C. 11th RFA received a message from 14th Infantry Bde, on their front line, requesting the batteries to continue a fast rate of fire on the left & spur FME 14 as at that point they were short of men. The B.C. fires in advance of their 4 rnds gun fire a frn which the former rate of fire was resumed.	
"	"	9.14p	About this time B.C.'s finding that the situation appeared to be quieter, allowed the rate of fire to slow down to new form to about sec fire 1 min.	
"	"	1.30p	This was continued until 10·0 pm when orders were received to reduce the rate of fire to RQ fire & ammunition.	
"	"	10.0 p.m	Both batteries ceased firing.	

NoB rounds fired 15th - 1485; 11th - 250.

HHS ft. Col

Army Form C. 2118.

Page 11

WAR DIARY
or
INTELLIGENCE SUMMARY.
(Erase heading not required.)

Place	Date	Hour	Summary of Events and Information	Remarks and references to Appendices
BRIELEN	14/7/15	3.30 a.m.	F.O.O. 10th Bty reported that 30 to 40 Germans were passing through Command trench N of FME 14 carrying sandbags.	
"	"	5.15 am	10th Bty fired a few rounds at "J".	
"	"	1.25 pm	" " turned on to FORTIN 17 at request of 146th Inf Bde.	
"	"	6.5	10th Bty turned on to pts "J" & "T" by C.R.A. fired rapid fire	
"	"	6.20	until 6.20 when ordered to cease fire.	
"	"	6.30 pm	11th Bty fired on Comm. Trench in rear of FME 14 & "T" at request of 148th Inf Bde. 5 rounds Bty fire was fired in retaliation for hostile fire in an Comm: Trenches.	
"	15/7/15		10th Bty registered during the afternoon. H.Q. dugouts were shelled with 10th Bty's Very Gun.	
"	16/7/15		Both batteries registered during the day. In the evening H.Q. were again shelled with Very gun so it was decided to move. Billets (temporary) were established at VLAMERTINGHE	
"	"	5.10 pm	H.Q. moved there in motor Rolls Royce and fired on C.R.A.'s order at a trench mortar located at	HWS Lt Col

Army Form C. 2118.

WAR DIARY
or
INTELLIGENCE SUMMARY.
(Erase heading not required.)

Page 12.

Places	Date	Hour	Summary of Events and Information	Remarks and references to Appendices
BRIELEN	16.7.16		C.13 b 10.10. Observation was difficult owing to the rain.	
"	"	6.0pm	11th Bty turned on to "T" by regmt. of 14th Hy Art. fired 6 rounds at thatched cottage suspected O.P	
VLAMERTINGHE	17/7/16		C.7.b.9.2. During the day the Regular Intelpats were now selecting new billets as the huts in VLAMERTINGHE was too far back & also out of the area of the 49th Division. After considerable trouble were eventually found area ELVERDINGHE to which H.Q. moved after midnight.	
ELVERDINGHE	"	12 noon	11th Bty fired 6 rounds on cross roads C.1.C.7.1. a supposed observing station. One direct hit was recorded.	
"	18.7.16	7.5pm	at 7.5pm major Bunce who was then F.O.O of 16th Bty noticed about 8 germans looking over "Boundary gate" behind "T"?	
"	"	7.8pm	16th Bty F.O.O noticed, about 500 × 700 × behind this gate, at about 16a 3.2 a line of german infantry entrenched advancing with their right on the trail behind this line he observed a second line moving in a N.W direction with their wing moving westwards.	HH Ath Lt Col

Army Form C. 2118.

WAR DIARY
or
INTELLIGENCE SUMMARY
(Erase heading not required.)

Page 13.

Place	Date	Hour	Summary of Events and Information	Remarks and references to Appendices
ELVERDINGHE	18/7/15	7.0 a.m	In rear troops seen missing behind hedges & amongst ruins etc. They seemed to come from lines surrounding FARM at C.8.a.5.2.	
"	"	7.10	A report was sent to C.R.A. & 11th R.F. wrote also to 14th infantry Bde & 3rd F.A. Bde. The 3rd F.A. Bde opened fire with considerable effect. The troops were seen in dark blue uniform & appeared to be of good physique. No attack was made.	
"	"	7.20 a.m	10th Bty fired 4 rounds in neighbourhood of "T".	
"	"	6.15 a.m	11th Bty fired a couple of rounds in Thatched Roof Wood in support of 148th Inf.	
"	"	7.30 a.m	Turned in to FME 14 at request of 148th Inf: R.F. C.R.A. sent a message to say that Brigade commander was very pleased with the report sent in by the F.O.O.s of the two Batteries — Major Duncan & Lieut Watts.	
"	19/7/15	5 am	11th R.F. fired 4 rounds at request of 148th Inf R.F.	
"	"	6.20 a.m	" " " " " FME 14	

MHA Lt. Col.

Army Form C. 2118.

Page 14

WAR DIARY
or
INTELLIGENCE SUMMARY.
(Erase heading not required.)

Place	Date	Hour	Summary of Events and Information	Remarks and references to Appendices
ELVERDINGHE	20.7.17	A.M.	During the morning a new German gun registered on trenches about F.M.E 14 & 'T'. It is estimated as being a 4.2" firing from direction of PILKEN.	
"	21.7.17 12noon		A few Germans were observed in the trenches at 'T' in with us trans round their caps. Spiked helmets	
"	10.15am		10th Battery fired at a section of Boches in the "Bowden gate at 'T'."	
"	"		Destroyed a suspected O.P at C2.C.3.2. with 3 direct hits & also registered a tram-sunken rd. on O.P at C 3 C 3 4.	
"	2.45pm		" " 147 a.nt 132.	
"	22.7.17 3.30p		10th Bty stand fire at C13 b 8.6 at near 3.30p.m. at rear of " Bowden gap at 'T'. Few rounds were fired.	
"	"	9.10am	11th Bty fired 5 rounds at 'T' in retaliation.	
"	"	4.10pm	" " " " " at suspected O.P area PILKEN	
"	22.7.	—	F.O.O 10th Bty reports that considerable work has been done behind "Bowden gap" at 'T'.	
"	"	3.30pm	10th Bty fired 2 rounds at working party behind "Bowden gap".	HRA/4. Col

1577 Wt. W10791/1773 500,000 1/15 D. D. & L. A.D.S.S./Forms/C. 2118.

WAR DIARY
or
INTELLIGENCE SUMMARY.

Army Form C. 2118.

Page 45

Place	Date	Hour	Summary of Events and Information	Remarks and references to Appendices
ELVERDINGHE	23.7.15	12 noon	11th Battery fired four rounds at "T" at request of 148th inf Bde.	
"	"	12.10 pm	wheather was at standstill.	
"	"	9.0 pm	11th inf. were this moved to A 23 d 7.4.	
"	24.7.15.	6.0 pm	Enemy reported to be working in trenches round & behind "Roemers Gab". 11th Bs attey fired two rounds at Roemers gab where there were a number of german infantry observed.	
"	25.7.15	9.30 a.m.	Enemy shelled TUGELA FME — 12 rounds fired. German infantry often observed in the Stern at C 7 b 10.0.1.	
"	"	12.15	C.R.A. turned 10th RFA a to howitzer two points C13 & 9.9 & C14 a 3.4. Difficult was first achieved with telephonic communication then a Thunderstorm came up owing to bad weather was experienced in ranging so that only 19 rounds were so fired instead of the allotment of 53.	
"	"	12.30	Ceased firing.	
"	26.7.15	2.16 pm	The 10th Battery fired 13 rounds at a redoubt C 7 b.1.1.	
"	"	5.15 pm	" — " B — " — "T" at request of 148th inf. bde.	

Army Form C. 2118.

Page 16.

WAR DIARY
or
INTELLIGENCE SUMMARY.
(Erase heading not required.)

Place	Date	Hour	Summary of Events and Information	Remarks and references to Appendices
ELVERDINGHE	27/7/15		The enemy kept up a slow rate of fire on our trenches almost all day.	
"	28/7/15	11.20am	The 18th Battery fired 6 rounds at a Barn (suspected O.P.) at C.2.c.3.4. obtaining an direct ht.	
"		2.0pm	11th Bty fired 5 rounds at "T" at revmt of 14th Bty Bde.	
"	29/7/15	3.30pm	11th " " 5 " at suspicious O.P. at C.2.c.3.2 in retaliation at revmt of 14th Bde Bty Bde.	
"	30/7/15 12.15p		Both batteries opened fire for 10 minutes on orders received from C.R.A. on enemy trenches in C.14.a.3.4, C.14.a.6.3, C.14.a.2.9. Number of rounds fired 34.	
"	31/7/15		Slight intermittent shelling by the Germans.	

H.H. Carr OR

Army Form C. 2118.

WAR DIARY
or
INTELLIGENCE SUMMARY.
(Erase heading not required.)

Confidential

War Diary

of

49th (W.R.) Divisional Ammunition Column

From 1st September 1915 to 30th September 1915

(Volume 1.)

www.ingramcontent.com/pod-product-compliance
Lightning Source LLC
Chambersburg PA
CBHW081547160426
43191CB00011B/1864